Home Is Everywhere

Adventures Of An Itinerant Homecare Nurse

Sylvia Talkington, RN

ISBN 978-1-957077-39-0

Publisher's Cataloging-in-Publication data

Names: Talkington, Sylvia G., author.
Title: Home is everywhere : adventures of an itinerant homecare nurse /
Sylvia G. Talkington.
Series: Simple Naturalist Series
Description: Littleton, CO: Simple Naturalist, 2023.
Identifiers: ISBN: 978-1-957077-39-0
Subjects: LCSH Talkington, Sylvia G. | Nurses--Biography. | Nursing. |
Nurses' writings. | BISAC BIOGRAPHY & AUTOBIOGRAPHY / Personal
Memoirs | BIOGRAPHY & AUTOBIOGRAPHY / Medical
Classification: LCC RT34 .T35 2023 | DDC 610.7306/9--dc23

Published by Simple Naturalist.

Publishing assistance by BookCrafters, Parker, Colorado.
www.bookcrafters.net

A house is made with walls and beams.

A home is made with love and dreams.

PREFACE

FROM 1990 THROUGH 2015 I visited over five hundred homes as a home healthcare nurse. In Four Canadian provinces, Puerto Rico, and every state but Alaska. It was a time when technology and medicine were revolutionizing healthcare by moving nursing care from the hospital to home. What I discovered were stories needing to be told. Stories of life and the human condition. The purpose of *Home is Everywhere* is to tell those stories, real stories about real people and situations. Contemporary references and cultural history and traditions are imbedded in each story. Hidden in this set of stories is the inference of the significance and necessity of human interaction through story.

Names of home healthcare agencies and staff have been changed as have patient names. Some events may have been enhanced but are accurate and based on facts at the time they took place. Home care nursing practice techniques are described in many stories, not for the purpose of teaching but related to situations that Americans may have had or will experience. *Home Is Everywhere* is NOT a nursing or home health nursing textbook or traditional memoir or autobiography. Although each story stands alone, there are overall themes of compassion and caring. I and my team of reviewers made every effort to see that each story is easy to read and as enjoyable as possible. Whether you read one story or more I hope you will discover how fragile life is and how much alike we really are. Each life story deserves to be told.

INTRODUCTION

TO BE TRUTHFUL, *Home is Everywhere* began when I was a kid. Even though I didn't know it. I was always a homebody. From sunrise to sundown playing in the playhouse my dad built when I was five. I always wanted to be a nurse. All the women in the family were nurses. I imagined travelling to homes in faraway lands. I fashioned a nursing cap from Dad's white handkerchief and marked it with a red lipstick cross to care for my dollies and flea-bitten black cat.

I traded that white handkerchief for a nursing cap and when I graduated from nursing school I intended to set out on adventures as a Maryknoll missionary nurse in Africa. The good Sisters, in their wisdom, thought it best I stay home. The Methodist missionary board wrote that wars in Congo and Biafra were too dangerous. Nurses were being called home.

So, I stayed home, got married, started a hospital intensive care unit, had kids, practiced as a critical care nurse, and wrote a nursing book or two. Health care was changing rapidly in the wake of burgeoning technology and medical firsts. The writing was on the wall; healthcare of the future would be centered in the home.

I dabbled in creative writing after a career laced with academic and technical writing – Course syllabi, training materials, nursing books, study reports, magazine articles, and freelance writing as owner of HealthWrite™.

What better way to jump into the world of creative writing than by attending my first American Association of Writers and

Writing Programs annual meeting in Seattle in 2014. I pitched the concept of the book to an editor from Hudson Whitman Press at Excelsior University in Albany NY and was ready to sign a contract. At the time they were publishing stories of nurses who had been deployed to Afghanistan. A plan to publish *Home Is Everywhere* launched.

When authors are interviewed about how long it took to write their book it's not uncommon to hear that it may have taken years. And so, it did. *Home Is Everywhere* sat idle during the nine years since, delayed by ill health. 2023 was the year. It was time. Material for stories that would ultimately become *Home is Everywhere* came from notes and scraps of paper that filled a four-drawer filing cabinet. What has kept me going has been the desire to finish the book. To let the stories be told. Reviewers have bolstered my determination. Most of all I've become a better writer and we laugh at how awful early stories were.

I would like to express my very sincere thanks to Paula and Ed Stearns, Carol Tagstrom, Cookie Knoll, Monika Nash, John Finch, and Rick Block for their contributions. A special thank you to Deb Zelkowitz who applied her editing skills for creating the final manuscript.

TABLE OF CONTENTS

1.   Mall People..1
2.   Becoming a Road Warrior...6
3.   In All Kinds of Weather...14
4.   Roses, Humming, and Slave Quilt............................21
5.   Tin Roof and Dirt Floor...30
6.   Pigeon With a Zip Code...38
7.   Ticks, Chicks, and Grasshoppers.............................48
8.   So, You're Black..56
9.   Pest Control...61
10. Finding Home...65
11. Broadleaf Maple Flag..72
12. Birdseed and Fancy Feast...78
13. Tasting Cultures...85
14. Brotherly Love..95
15. Animal Encounters...101
16. Humility at Gate 77..108
17. Keebler Elves Keep Watch..112
18. Everyone Needs a Spot..118
19. What Wreath Are You..124

1 Mall People

Those who have little give much.

I'M NOT SURE ANYONE KNOWS where Ralph's chili comes from. But every Thursday at precisely 10:30 a.m. you'll find Ralph on the 16th Street Mall ladling thick red chili into paper bowls from a battered enamelware pot. Vince, manager at Dairy Queen, provides plastic spoons. 16th Street Pedestrian Mall opened in 1982, linking Uptown (Capitol area, Denver Library and Art Museum) to Lower Downtown and Union Station. Every five minutes a free Mall Shuttle bus going Uptown passes the shuttle going Downtown. Buses stop at corners where passengers hop on and off on their way to offices, retail stores, restaurants, fast foods, bars, and souvenir shops. A common area runs the full length of the Mall. White plastic lawn chairs and cement benches provide an area where Mall People play Monopoly, *shoot the breeze*, solve Word Search puzzles, and eat lunch. At Curtis Street an old upright piano, recently painted psychedelic colors, attracts various keyboard artists. Some days it's jazz, some days classical, and sometimes it's two friends plunking out *Heart and Soul*. Brendan Callahan fiddles Irish reels and ballads at Stout Street near an Irish pub. Passersby stop to listen and go away with tears in their eyes. He could be an Irish Rover he's so talented. The Pencil Guy sits on the sidewalk in front of Famous Footwear with his ceramic mug of #2s nicely sharpened and pant legs folded beneath him. Trees planted along the Mall have matured.

Several of my home care patients live downtown so I visit the Mall often, getting to know Street People regulars. I enjoy talking with them. Most have had very interesting and surprising lives. Lives that haven't always been easy or kind.

You know when Ralph is out and about. You can hear the hum of his motorized wheelchair. You'll also recognize the thickly bandaged legs and feet with purple toes sticking out. Ralph is unable to take more than a few painful steps because of chronic venous stasis ulcers. In plain language blood in the veins of the lower legs becomes sluggish causing marked swelling. Sometimes ulcers *weep* clear fluid and require regular wound care with gauze dressings to keep them from becoming infected. When ulcers aren't infected dressings can be changed once or twice a month. When the ulcers become infected, they require changing three times a week. Sometimes daily for seven days. Here's the problem we faced. When ulcers are infected the payer changes from Medicaid to Medicare. Medicare requires a person stay home for the entire 60-day certification period. Except for medical appointments, the patient can't leave home. Agencies are being heavily fined for not meeting this requirement. It's a constant dilemma. More like an ongoing argument. Keeping Ralph at home so an infection can clear has been almost impossible at times. A few times I've had to insist on switching to Medicare.

"You know Ralph if we don't get this infection under control you're going to be sitting with The Pencil Guy. Or worse." I threaten him.

"OK," he pouts. "I'll find someone for Thursdays."

On occasions he's homebound he sits in his third-floor window at Halcyon House looking down at the Mall. Friends wave and share Mall and Street news via pantomime. He gestures the number of days he has left to endure.

"It's all your fault," he says to me. "Pure torture. Like a cage. I guess there's one positive: I'm free in two weeks. Good thing; just in time for Halloween. I'm going to Trick or Treat on the Mall as *The Mummy*. I already have the leg bandages."

Sixty days are almost over. The ulcers are healing nicely. The infection has cleared. I see him out on the Mall the next week, a week earlier than his release date. Reluctantly, I've switched back to Medicaid. He could have benefited from finishing out the sixty days. I was lucky to get him to stay put for four weeks.

"At least promise me you'll lie down and elevate your legs for at least an hour a day. Staying up all day makes them so much worse. How long have you been up today?"

"Naw, haven't been up too long."

"You know I can tell when you're fibbing. All I have to do is look at the swelling and dressings."

"Well, maybe just don't look down at my legs. Maybe I wear a lap blanket. Maybe you can just say you didn't see me here. Right? Want a bowl of chili?"

Mall People lunch elsewhere on Monday, Tuesday, Wednesday, and Friday. Sandwiches are distributed at St. Elizabeth's at noon Monday through Friday. The Salvation Army serves a warm meal daily at 11am. Fr. Woody at Holy Ghost has hot soup available all day.

Most of my patients live in subsidized low-income apartments at Halcyon House on the corner of the Mall at Arapahoe Street. One of Colorado's success stories of de-institutionalization is twenty-four-year-old Steve Summers, born with cerebral palsy, who has his own apartment and works at Tattered Cover Bookstore Downtown. Steve's apartment is sparsely furnished to accommodate his mobility needs. He walks with elbow crutch canes and is quite mobile. A fireman's pole from ceiling to floor is positioned next to his mattress on the floor. He rises from the mattress to standing by pulling up the pole with his arms. Each morning a caregiver visits for four hours; helping him shower and dress for work, preparing meals, grocery shopping, housekeeping, and laundry. I visit monthly to do a health and wellness check. Last month he showed me scabs on both elbows and a cut on his knee.

"Ouch, Steve, what happened?" He rarely falls and is a pro getting up and down curbs, on and off buses and walking on a sidewalk alongside others.

"I was coming out of Halcyon and one of those little yip-yip dogs was off leash. Just as I stepped out, he ran in front of me. His owner was chasing him so fast she's the one who knocked me down."

Stella, Steve's eighty-one-year-old neighbor is currently receiving blood thinner injections for ten days. That gives me time to make a quick stop on the Mall to say hello to everyone. Steve has become Stella's adopted grandson. Sometimes Steve's girlfriend shares an evening meal or watches a movie on CD with them.

Street People of 16TH Street Mall are a community. A tight knit neighborhood of friends who treat one another with dignity. Everyone helps each other. They have little and give much. I'm ashamed for the times I've referred to Halcyon House as Hell House. It's not the upper rent district and like all aging buildings maintenance is often long overdue. But it's home.

This isn't the first time I've made home care visits in this area. While working at National Jewish Hospital in 1990 I was recruited to volunteer at Stout Street homeless clinic on Saturdays. In 1989 Mother Theresa of Calcutta visited Denver and announced she was sending her Daughters of Charity to Denver to assist with the AIDs crisis.

"I have a gift for you.... I will give you my sisters and I hope that, together, we are going to do something beautiful for God," stated Mother Theresa's announcement to the *Rocky Mountain News*.

The first group of Sisters moved into Seton House in January 1990. It had been renovated from a Catholic high school to a residence for the sisters and hospice care for AIDS patients. One summer Saturday the Clinic received a call from Seton house.

4

"Mother Superior wonders if one of the volunteers might be free to sit with a hospice patient." I was more than happy to help. We'd seen most of the drop-ins at the clinic and I didn't mind walking the two blocks to Seton House. Mother met me at the door.

"Thank you. I'm glad you were able to come. You'll be doing something beautiful today. Jack has no one." He has pneumocystis pneumonia and is in the early stages of dying. His parents have abandoned him, and his partner Pat is grieving and unwell. "They live at Halcyon House. Jack is all alone."

In those early years when AIDS was a curse the Sisters carried on, holding the dying in their loving care. What did Jack see when he closed his eyes at the end? Sister's beautiful smiling face. I only made that one visit. 1990 was the first year I started home healthcare nursing and spent the rest of my life in homes everywhere.

2 Becoming A Road Warrior

Oh! The Places You'll Go
— Dr. Suess

WHEN MY WORK REQUIRED OUT-OF-STATE TRAVEL, beginning in 2001, adventure also became my life. Jobs fill your pockets, but adventures fill your soul. Travel is in my DNA. I easily settled into the life of a woman business traveler for fifteen years. I think of travel as an occupation that requires a sense of humor, a lot of flexibility and a positive attitude. Travelers who survive are the ones who design travel routines that keep them healthy, happy, and sane. I didn't just survive—I bloomed. I credit it to a few habits that worked.

I was loyal to one airline and enrolled in that airline's frequent flier mileage rewards program. For many flights if the primary airline doesn't fly to a particular city they partner with another airline as a code share. Every flight I reserved a specific seat assignment – mid-cabin, Row 17 or 18, window seat on the left side, if traveling West; window seat on the right side, if traveling East. Guaranteed best scenic view from 35,000 feet. Being in a window seat necessitated carrying a 12-pack of pocket Kleenex. Middle seat passengers, at least those who always seemed to sit next to me, without fail, coughed, and sneezed on me and wiped their dripping noses on their sleeve-- year-round; allergies, flu, common colds. To get to the lavatory, I learned to somewhat gracefully climb over passengers B and C who were engrossed in a movie, sleeping on their tray table, or writing a year-end earnings report. What to say about the lavatory? I had nightmares about being locked in or sucked down and out to the wild blue yonder.

I never signed up for airline brand credit cards that gave miles for purchases. Travelers who earned miles other than by flying, were looked upon as traitors. I learned to sleep anywhere anytime — upright in a chair, on a couch in a hotel lobby, against an exit window or snoozing on my tray table. Sleeping on the floor in the gate area is far preferable to snaking around those miserable metal arms on bench seats. Pillows on planes were still available without cost. Imagine that! I was fine with a rolled-up jacket or sweater. Poofy neck pillows were fashionable but rarely worn by business travelers. I invested in a good pair of noise-reduction headphones and carried a six-outlet power strip in my briefcase. Yes, it's true that airport terminals were notorious for a scarcity of power outlets. The lucky person locating a wall outlet became a best friend to five others.

I learned the hard way that carry-on bags will be checked to your destination (against your will) IF you don't follow the requirements — 22"x14"x9," whether soft-sided athletic bag or roller bag with telescoping handle. I kept a wallet with identification and emergency info, boarding pass, and cell phone in a cross-body bag instead of a purse. A 5x7 inch lined spiral notepad went with me everywhere, ready at an instant to document something that caught my eye. All those somethings came to be this book.

As a person who hates shopping for clothing, what to wear and pack was a bit of a problem. The main objective was to reflect a business style. Purchasing a black suit with appropriate blouses was painful but necessary. When traveling to colder locations I wore light wool cardigan sweaters and wool dress pants. I packed only two work outfits for a single trip — one set suitable for making home visits and one for meeting with the administrators, owners, and directors of the home care agency. The only jewelry I wore were simple post pearl earrings and stylish and colorful lapel pins. Following Secretary of State Madeline Albright's example, I chose pins that made for starting an interesting conversation. No one needs more than two pairs of shoes that are, above all, comfortable – dress and casual. One pair of jeans and a knit shirt fit for after-hours roll up nicely for packing. Super large Ziplocs kept everything flat and compact. I never got used to winter travel with coats, hats, scarves, gloves and boots. My abiding rule: if it won't all fit in the carry-on, leave the offending item home.

I made sure to have an extra phone charger, battery-operated flashlight (before smart phone flashlights) and small first aid kit easily accessible.

My best strategy to escape the chaos and noise pollution of airport terminals was retreating to the chapel with its guaranteed peace and quiet. I found that airport chapels were a study in world religions. In Minneapolis I observed an orthodox Rabbi in a prayer shawl facing the direction of the Wailing Wall, a Muslim man unrolling a prayer rug to face Mecca, a Tibetan monk meditating in the lotus position, an Episcopal priest in a black cassock and white clerical collar reading his pocket Bible, and a religious Sister praying the rosary. All at the same time.

It was a couple of years before it occurred to me that I spent more time in a hotel room than my condo back home. I also realized that if I chose one hotel chain and learned their brands, I could go to sleep in a familiar bedroom every night. I inhabited my room like I lived at home, and it looked like it. I transformed every hotel room into a happy place by filling the ice bucket with a bouquet of fresh flowers for the duration of the stay. I collected unused complimentary shampoos, soaps, and lotions and put them to good use by donating them to the homeless shelter back home. The moment I unlocked the hotel door and put the luggage inside I located every exit route and fire extinguisher. I was picky about where my room was in the hotel. I always booked a room on an upper floor, away from elevators and at the end of the hall. On occasion I heard someone slide a card key and attempt to open the door in the middle of the night. Oops, a sleepy night desk person forgot to re-key the card or keyed two cards with the same number.

I started a hobby of collecting plastic key cards for the grandchildren who used them to play a matching game. Can you believe I sent postcards in the early years to each grandchild so they would know where I was? I was a happy hotel guest by being thoughtful and considerate. It's quite simple. I greeted housekeeping employees by name and thanked them. I left the maid a tip on the bedside table when checking out. There were always special employees everywhere. Everyone knew Melvin, senior doorman at a Hilton Garden Inn in Houston. He made everyone's day because every afternoon he mixed the most delicious fresh fruit infusions for guests. We had something to look forward to in addition to his smiling face at the end of our workday. And he was always ready to listen.

Most of my colleagues who traveled continued their exercise programs using the hotel gym or membership in a gym with nationwide locations. My exercise was walking every day. I would check with front desk personnel about safe and scenic walking areas nearby, letting them know where I was going and approximately how long I'd be gone. On more than one occasion it proved valuable. Like the time when the park where I walked was farther away than I was told. I lingered to watch the sunset and I got lost on the way back.

"Hey there, Ms. Talkington, just checking in to see if you're OK. Want our shuttle to come pick you up?"

Except for a few occasions in NYC, when I used a car service or subway, it was necessary to rent a car every trip. I chose a rental car for its safety, size, and road service, based on the terrain and distances I needed to drive. No subcompact if I was going to be driving in winter weather, long distances, or to states with high rates of road rage. What changed my mind happened in Texas where two half-ton Ram pickups played *let's pin the little Fiat between us.*

It's impossible to rent a car without having to suffer through the Rental Car Shuttle bus experience to get to and from the terminal and off- airport lots. It is quite a comedy. As riders rush to get in first, those of us who always ended up standing in the shuttle aisle became skilled at keeping our carry-ons between our legs while holding the overhead strap.

Over fifteen years I found that fellow travelers built recognizable friendships especially if they consistently traveled to the same places on the same schedules. We became a band of brothers and sisters who understood the rigors and situations, laughing about how long we'd be able to keep it up; some of us five days a week fifty weeks a year.

It took a few months before I got used to eating out every day. I never minded eating alone. Some colleagues never ate out alone but ordered room service unless we were together as a group. On very few occasions I ordered room service. I love breakfast so I chose hotels with the best full-service breakfast bars. Although I'm not a morning person it was fun sitting at the community table and having someone to say good morning to over scrambled eggs.

When onsite at agencies I usually grabbed lunch at a relatively healthy and recognizable fast-food restaurant, if possible. In smaller towns the agency staff were excited there was a visitor so they could special order a favorite like Dairy Queen or Sonic. Subway, Chick-fil-A, Panera, or Qdoba became standard go-tos when I was in the suburbs. When I retired, I swore I would never eat at Panera's for the rest of my life. Many days I ate take-out while reviewing patient records. By the end of the day, I felt entitled to have a good evening meal. And I did.

Above all else, to ensure a relaxing and enjoyable dinner I did not allow the host to seat me in the back of the restaurant by the bathrooms or kitchen. They tried. Why do they only do that to women as if a woman eating alone needs to be hidden away?

It wasn't long before I compiled a list of airport food court favorites. In small towns, I ate where the locals ate. The local hometown favorite was recognizable by pot roast and cherry pie on the menu. On a blustery September night, I had pizza with the Gallipolis Ohio football team.

Air travel wouldn't be what it is without delays and surprises. Only once was I truly frightened by an inflight event. It was a familiar route home to Denver from Dallas and always turbulent. That night wasn't any different. *"Strange,"* I thought as I watched the sunset. I could swear I recognized the San Luis Valley below. It wasn't on the route.

"This is your captain speaking. As some of you may have noticed we've taken a detour over the mountains and been put into a holding pattern over Alamosa and Monte Vista."

Lights from towns in the valley passed below *again*. Our small regional jet with 70 passengers had been holding for over two hours. The flight attendant served one free alcoholic beverage to calm the frustration. Passengers shared snacks they brought on-board and airline snacks ran out somewhere over the Valley.

"This is your co-captain speaking. We are low on fuel so we're diverting to Colorado Springs to refuel. Denver is still on a ground hold for lightening."

The refueling crew was waiting to hook up when we landed in the Springs, when from the back of the plane a man yelled,

"I want off!! I have a right to get off. I want to see the captain!"

The cabin door opened, and the co-pilot walked down the aisle to negotiate. He rolled his eyes at me as he re-entered the cockpit. Air Traffic controllers in Denver and Colorado Springs were notified. Finally, United Headquarters gave us a go ahead. We had a thirty-minute window to take off for Denver. The co-pilot escorted the passenger to an exit door in the galley. As he walked to the waiting van the passenger announced, "I want my luggage. I demand you get it."

The co-pilot was standing in front of me (I was in seat 1A). "Oh shit. This guy is crazy. What an asshole. Oh, Ma'am please excuse me." He turned lobster red.

United headquarters was again contacted and gave approval. A baggage handler arrived in rain gear. The baggage hold was opened, the bag identified and retrieved just as the co-pilot came screaming out of the cockpit and leaned out the galley exit. "STOP STOP STOP!!!" he yells through the rain. We're in the middle of refueling. Shut off the fuel, disconnect and back up. Close the baggage hold immediately!"

He supervises. We were running out of time. Finally, once the baggage compartment was closed the fuel crew reattached and finished. Looking calm and business as usual, the co-pilot returned to the cockpit after securing the galley exit door. The flight attendant announces,

"All right, everyone, prepare the cabin for take-off. Looks like we've been cleared to take off for landing in Denver."

It's a 30-minute flight; an up-down as it's called. Seconds after takeoff as the landing gear is folding into the hold the cabin glows with heat. We all start madly feeling the walls and under the seats for where it's coming from. Straining to see out the windows we look for fire or smoke.

"Co-pilot here. Your flight attendant has alerted us to the rising temperature in the cabin. We've investigated it, and it looks like we took a flock of birds in the right engine. Just to be safe we've shut it down. We're perfectly fine with just one engine."

I closed my eyes and visualized a headline: *Small jet with 70 aboard lands safely in Denver after taking a flock of birds in the right engine*. I try not to think about what has happened when small planes take a flock in the engine. On the ground at last, bedraggled passengers with frayed nerves, like me, make our way toward the terminal.

The next day I cajole my way into talking with United's President by saying, "I'm a dedicated United flyer with 800,000 lifetime miles and I want to speak to you about the situation last Friday night aboard Dallas flight 1028 to Denver. The co-pilot deserves a medal."

3 In All Kinds of Weather

Neither snow nor rain nor heat nor gloom

HAS BEEN SYNONYMOUS with the tireless work the U.S. Postal Service does to make sure you get your junk mail. In truth there is no official motto. How about a vote for making it the motto of home healthcare nurses? Nurses everywhere have their own weather experiences depending on where they're geographically located.

Life is one big adventure, full of storms, metaphorically speaking. Cataclysmic storms are the stuff that movie heroes face. For example, in the film Willow 2 from Disney Plus, a constant and ominous maelstrom darkens every scene. Then there's Bilbo Baggins of Hobbit fame who battled stone giants during a violent thunderstorm. Star Wars' The Force combines whirlwind and lightning. Even Homer's hero Odysseus was beset by storms.

Hurricanes

By 1900 the Bering Glacier in what would become Alaska had begun to shrink. In September 1900, newly arrived immigrants at the port of Galveston camped on the beaches, welcoming the bath water temperature waves coming ashore. On Friday, September 7th, Isaac Cline, physician, government appointed weatherman in Texas, and a pioneer scientist in climatology, couldn't sleep. Something seemed terribly wrong. It would be called the Great Galveston Hurricane. Officially there were 8,000 dead and 10,000 homeless. It was the deadliest natural disaster in United States history. Clara Barton, a nurse, and founder of the Red Cross, traveled to Galveston at 78 years old to direct what we now call disaster relief. Known as the Angel of the Civil War Battlefield, she was dispatched from Washington D.C. to administer and oversee the distribution of relief monies and supplies. FEMA was born.

When Hurricane Katrina made landfall on August 29th, 2005, I was standing in front of physicians at East Texas Cardiology group in Tyler, Texas. They're polite and tolerate my introduction to remote telemonitoring. Yet, they're skeptical of infringement on their territory. I'm anxious to wind this up. It's' late afternoon. Something seems terribly wrong. It's eerily quiet.

That's weird, I think, as I pull into the hotel parking lot. It's full of cars. A note from the office is taped on my door. *Please come to the office as soon as possible. Phone service might be interrupted.* Unlocking the door to my room to drop off my briefcase, I'm a bit confused.

"So sorry, I must have the wrong room," I say apologetically.

Four-year-old Benny LaForce is bouncing on the bed, my bed, while his sister Adrienne is flipping through channels trying to find Mister Rogers. Nothing is on but news bulletins. Mrs. LaForce crashes out of the bathroom when Benny shrieks.

"Stranger danger !!@"

When I reach the office, staff try not to be as frantic as they look. The lobby crowd is restless, some are crying, some are angry, some are just scared, most are exhausted. Shocking stories filter among the milling groups.

"A hurricane hit New Orleans this morning. People are fleeing east to Houston for shelter," says the desk clerk looking at me while silently thinking *where have you been lady?*

"Looks like we won't need to ask you to share your room. The La Forces were able to share a double room with friends. Housekeeping will bring you fresh sheets and towels."

Next day I had just enough gasoline to make it to Houston at a snail's pace. New Orleans did not receive a direct hit, but major damage was done when the levees protecting the city collapsed under the weight of the rain and storm surge. By August 30th 80 percent of the city is underwater. Numbers later confirmed that 770,000 people were displaced, Seventy percent were 60 years and older. Many neighborhoods were eradicated, including 68 nursing homes. One of our home care agencies in New Orleans lost over two hundred monitors, floating in the muck around the city. It took almost six months to reinstall fifty new monitors by the time we located patients who had been displaced and finally had electricity.

Katrina set in motion what would become mandatory Emergency Preparedness. In the six months following Katrina, billions of dollars flooded states with monies to develop and implement Emergency Preparedness practices. Home healthcare nurses' daily lives changed immediately as the first Emergency Preparedness rules and regulations were put into law. Agency owners and staff were expected to implement within six months the new rules governing how to prepare for hurricanes and other weather-related disasters. Radio stations were assigned as emergency alert systems (EAS), counties and cities were evaluated for risk potential for weather hazards. Mandatory evacuation routes were designated, criteria were developed for sheltering in place to address the universal problem of residents refusing to leave their homes. Finally, rudiments of a coordinated national plan emerged. Telecommunication systems were updated to link cities, counties, states, and federal agencies. Emergency Preparedness has tripled with the increase in numbers of weather-related hazards and disasters. Each year an agency must create an Emergency Preparedness Plan specific to the agency. Hurricanes I encountered that affected home care visits: Florida (3), Louisiana (3) North Carolina (4), and Virginia (5).

Tornadoes

We've finished a one-day staff training session at Greenwood Home Care in Mississippi. They've elected to participate in a home care study conducted by the University where I work. Clouds are turning a sickly green and faded purple. A haunting silence and stillness hovers everywhere. As warily navigate down a two-lane county road, driving south from Greenwood, the radio station's gospel music cuts out.

"**GZOOT, GZOOT, GZOOT** – This is WRGM emergency broadcasting network. Tornado warnings are in place for La Force county, Yazoo county, Washington county, Humphries county, and Sunflower county including the towns of Cleveland, Greenwood, Indianola, Leland, and Belzoni. Take cover immediately. Repeat, take cover immediately."

This announcement cycles every thirty seconds. I have no idea what county I'm in. I know I've just left Greenwood and I recognize town names on signs as they pass by. What county are they in? There's s no shoulder on these narrow roads, only deep ditches on each side. I'm trying to remember what to do. Get out and get down low. OK, go for the ditch. I start to open the door until I look out. That won't work. Like wooden soldiers at attention, a line of electric poles stands upright in the ditch and disappears over the horizon. I'm not enthusiastic about being electrocuted when the tornado blows them down on top of me. Don't panic, don't panic! I look out the back window and there *IT* is. I tuck my head onto my chest and slither down against the floorboard on the passenger side. Maybe I'll get sucked up into the tornado's eye, car and all. Sneaking a peek again, I can't believe it. I see the whirling funnel touch the ground several times as it disappears behind me. Tornadoes I encountered that affected home care visits: Alabama (2), Arkansas (1), Iowa (2), Kansas (1), (Oklahoma (3), Texas, Iowa (2.)

A Windstorm Called Haboob

Driving from Phoenix Sky Harbor airport to Tucson is usually a pleasant drive. Wispy cirrus clouds resembling Jane Austin's quill pen drift across broad blue skies. Not today. Without realizing what's happening I squint at the road ahead. Dust? Maybe a dirt devil like I've seen on many dry land farms on the plains. Land is being gobbled up and disappearing in front of me. There is no discernable horizon anywhere. Whatever it is, it's coming my way with a deafening roar that leaves my ears ringing. As my car is disappearing, it's as if I'm being drawn on a conveyor belt through a fiery furnace of dust against my will. I take a deep breath and hold it. What a stupid thing to do! Is this the Apocalypse? The Rapture? Oh heavens! Is it the way to……..? I haven't keeled over from holding my breath and whatever it was had veered east. There's grit in my teeth and sand in my hair.

"Did you get caught in the haboob yesterday?" is the first thing Nan, the Nursing Director, asks. "Now you can say you've seen one," she teases.

Haboobs are oppressive winds bringing sand from a desert. Who would have guessed Arizona had such things. Don't they belong in the Sahara? I encountered three haboobs while visiting agencies in Phoenix and Tucson.

Earthquakes

Earthquakes happen continuously in California and are measured on the Richter Scale, a seismographic scale expressing magnitude. Destructive quakes typically have magnitudes of 5.5 and 8.9. The Richter Scale is primarily effective for measuring regional earthquakes of less than 5.5. Moment Magnitude measurements are more effective for measuring large earthquakes. Most Californians, unless they're near the epicenter, never notice them. California was one of the states in my territory. Surely, I must have felt one having been to so many cities more than once. Number of Cities where I encountered earthquakes: Calabasas (1), Los Angeles (2), San Bernardino (1), San Francisco Bay (2)

Lightning

In the southwest tip of Texas, the cities of Pharr, Harlingen, Edinburg, and McAllen crowd into a quad city adjacent to the Rio Grande River on its final stretch to Brownsville before it empties into the Gulf of Mexico. Anytime I'm scheduled to visit one of those cities I can't wait to drive to South Padre Island where I stay. It's worth the forty-minute drive. Famous for white sandy beaches, spring break rendezvous, and winter getaways, South Padre boasts three hundred days of sunshine a year and calm weather during breezy summer days.

"Back to the Valley again Ms. Talkington?" asks Lincoln at the beachfront Holiday Inn check-in. "Good to see you. We have your usual room; top floor, away from elevators facing the beach. How was the drive from Harlingen?"

"Not the sunny drive I'm used to. An unfriendly breeze was picking up at Port Isabel and it started to rain over the causeway."

"Heavy rain just started coming down here. Let Gary get your luggage from the car."

It's not going to be the customary sunset from the balcony with cheese and crackers and a glass of wine. Laguna Madre Bay and the Gulf have completely disappeared. Might as well unpack. Somewhere between changing into jeans and a T shirt and putting cosmetics in the vanity the lights go out and the bathroom room door slams shut. Then, plate glass in the sliding balcony door blasts onto the bed and shards twinkle in the carpet.

Emergency lighting comes on in the hall and I head for the green EXIT sign. It takes all my strength against the wind to open the solid steel door fire exit. I'm not prepared. It's an outdoor escape stairway. Yikes! One mis-step will launch me eight floors below. Lightning is bolting everywhere, striking the hotel next door. Far out in the Gulf, sheet lightning is illuminating angry waves as guests reach shelter in the lobby at the end of their climb down the steps. Imaginary sea monsters appear in the Gulf, far in the distance. Lightning storms I encountered that affected visits, are too many to count.

4 Roses, Humming and Slave Quilt

Bringing Telehealth to the South

IT SEEMS WE AMERICANS have inventiveness in our blood, unleashed after trading a worn and oppressed life in one country for adventure and creativity in a new. Out of necessity, newfound freedoms, protected by revolution, spawned a civilization of expansion and growth. A frenetic pace ensued marked by inventions to match industrialization. And war. By end of April 1865 a president was dead. As were 720,000 soldiers, black and white. A shaky but intact union picked itself up off the battlefields. Some would later document that one of the primary determinants of the war was the telegraph.

With a tk tk, tickety tick, tick tickety tick of a wire transmitting code from one location to another, Lincoln was in full command of unruly and arguing generals. Not from a tent on the battlefield but the world's first war room. An enslaved people were free. Tickety-tick was only a set of varying vibrations. But what if there was a way to transmit human voice over the wires.?

The answer came in 1876 at Philadelphia as Alexander Graham Bell transmitted words to his partner Thomas Watson using a wire strung across a room. From then on, everything changed and tele became a prefix of what was to come.

One hundred and thirty years later I'm bringing a descendant of the telegraph and telephone with me to the South – Telemedicine.

Not from a war room to battlefields, but from medical centers to country hospitals tele is evolving.

I never experienced such heat. Sweltering, that's what they call it. I'm overcome. Swooning, not from anticipating a romantic land of mossy oak trees, but from sweating because of a muggy reality. White girl welcomed into a strange country. I admit it's the place. I'm overcome by history, people, traditions that draw me here. Crossing the Mississippi River and Mason Dixon line for the first time, I would be visiting, not antebellum homes, but homes of the elderly and poor. I'm here to bring remote telemonitoring, a spin-off of telemedicine.

Telemedicine started in a few states in the late sixties, making it possible for doctors to provide medical and psychiatric consultation to prisoners. It was too great a risk and too costly to transport felons from state and federal penitentiaries to a large city where specialists practiced. Soon, telemedicine proved to be even more beneficial in providing consultative medical care to communities without a doctor or access to specialists. A national model called *hub-spoke* was used to link the specialists at a large hospital or medical center to doctors and patients in small regional hospitals. Weekly clinics were scheduled via a video link between the two locations using a T1 line: a cable of wires with a lot of bandwidth to accommodate the video and audio.

Remote telemonitoring was naturally suited to home health care. Nurses would know every day, through data submitted from a home, if they should visit their patient that day or wait till the next scheduled visit.

Barbara, the nursing supervisor at Grace Home Health, is driving me to home visits. I'm spellbound. Flashbacks of 1960s Civil Rights Movement news coverage is much different from the landscape I see out the window.

"This is historic Mound Bayou," she says. "Don't blink. Hasn't grown all that much. It was founded by slaves in 1887 as the first all-black independent community in the South. Several of our patients live in the area."

Out the car window, buildings, cemeteries, and churches decrease in number and are replaced with commercial catfish ponds where a cotton field with a rusted cotton gin still stands guard. A mighty river, wider than I've ever seen, is in the distance.

"You don't see any nursing homes, do you?" Barbara asks.

"No. No I don't. Why is that?"

"In smaller towns, relatives, friends, and neighbors take care of the elderly. It's a given. They wouldn't think of doing things differently. It's part of our culture."

I couldn't have imagined that day, the many oral histories, and personal narratives I'd hear while bringing remote telemonitoring to the South.

A profusion of yellow climbing roses is clinging to a white picket fence. An ecstasy of scent from creeping white jasmine flowers encloses a tiny frame house in cool floral obscurity.

"Miss Jasmine will answer the door for us. She knows we're coming." Barbara touches my arm, nodding toward the front door.

A diminutive woman of indeterminate age appears at the door. The sweetest of shy smiles meets our hellos. Scanning my notes. Ah, must be the patient's daughter. Age forty-four. Next of kin.

"Oh, the flowers are heavenly, a sight to behold every year, Miss Jasmine!" compliments Barbara.

I learn later that thirty-eight years have gone by since this house first welcomed that smile. The story of how Miss Jasmine came to live here goes like this:

"Lawdy, now who done put that pore li'l white chile on them steps? Wass your name? Where you be from? Where's your momma?"

The same sweet shy smile that met ours, met Hattie Wilson's raised eyebrows as she entered First Baptist Church that day long ago. Hattie, being the first to arrive for Sunday worship one late Spring day, hastily called a meeting of church sisters.

"Now, just *what* is to be done?" boomed Miss Hattie, pointing at the group so fiercely her pink feathered hat almost fell off.

That day Miss Effie spoke only once. Not a woman to use an abundance of words, when she stood up the whispering silenced and people listened.

"I done raised my own. We needs each other. She's no pore li'l white chile, she's my sweet li'l Jasmine." Church sisters were relieved. Pastor Turner used the event to call forth scripture on the following Sunday.

Here she is at the door today, just as happy as if she were sitting on Miss Effie's lap in a new poplin dress that Sunday after she was abandoned. Miss Effie was fifty-five and Jasmine was four.

In 1946 children born with Mongolism, as it was properly called then, were often quietly cared for in state institutions for the rest of their lives. Attending school would never have been discussed. Considered *retarded* by common folk, Jasmine would have spent her life with other unfortunate orphans with birth injuries, brain deformities, or conditions we didn't have a clue about. Miss Effie saw to it that Jasmine was not a shut-in, kept home, away from public view because of looking strange and presumed to be *not quite right in the head*.

Townspeople were her family and Miss Effie replaced the mother she'd never remember. The outdoors and Miss Effie's teachings about God's creatures and people was a school without walls. She learned the alphabet, read *Dick and Jane*, dressed, and cuddled her dolls. She learned love and joy, kindness and patience and thanksgiving. Each morning they prayed with bowed heads. After supper they listened to the radio, recited psalms, and looked at photos in *Life* magazine till bedtime. Their weeks were busy. They shopped in town on Saturday. Attended church services on Sunday and welcomed visitors on Sunday afternoons. Wednesday was bible study; Thursday was choir practice. That was her life. Each year they planted and tended a large vegetable garden of sweet potatoes, okra, black-eyed peas, mustard, turnip and collard greens that were perfect to be cooked with the pork belly Clarence Davis gave them every year. Neighbors came to visit on muggy afternoons. Children grew up and moved to the city; got married and had babies. Over the years they all came back to visit. Jars of canned piccalilli and wild mayhaw jelly went with them when they left.

Six years ago, at eighty-seven, Miss Effie had a stroke from which she limped with a dead right side. Three years later a second stroke sent her to rest in her bed permanently. Together each morning they still began their day in prayer. Jasmine tenderly bathed and dressed Miss Effie, then slowly and delicately fed her grits with sips of chicory coffee. While Miss Effie napped, Jasmine tended the garden and clipped roses for the bedside table. At lunch she told Miss Effie about how blue the sky was or confirmed that rain was brewing in the afternoon clouds. Shirley Davis's funny little dog Jack was forever getting loose and sneaking over to Miss Effie's porch swing. They laughed at whatever mischief he was in to. Jasmine sat in wonder as Miss Effie retold familiar bible verses.

"Tell me again how it was when you were a little girl." Jasmine never tired of listening to stories of strange historical events. They'd often reminisce about various birthdays, holidays, and townsfolk predicaments, as Miss Effie called them. Although darkness had overtaken her vision, the cataracts did not dim her memory.

Elders and Sisters from the church again began whispering about *what was to be done…*

So, here we are on the front porch to suggest an answer for what could be done. Just as Miss Effie had posed a solution to a problem so long ago. Now, the solution is remote telemonitoring. One of the largest home health agencies in four counties purchased several remote telemonitoring units. I'm here to show staff how the units work and how monitoring can help their patients.

Not far in the future, remote monitoring would become web based. Information once relayed from a home to a Central Station in the agency office will be sent to a nurse's tablet. Within a short number of years, remote monitoring would become cyberbased where information from a home would be transmitted directly to a nurse's smart watch. Just as it was in those early days when remote telemonitoring became an indispensable tool in everyday healthcare in the home.

At the time I was in Mississippi, a remote monitoring unit was a small clock-radio-sized device. A blood pressure cuff, finger clip to measure oxygenation and a floor scale were attached to the back of the monitor by cables. Every day, at a preset time, the device would visually and verbally cue the patient to step on the scale, sit down, put on the blood pressure cuff and finger clip. Sit quietly and let it do its thing. When it finished, readings displayed on the device's face and a voice inside the box proceeded to ask a series of preset yes/no questions. Questions were set by the homecare nurse based on a person's symptoms or diagnoses. The patient, or helper, pressed green 'yes' or red 'no' soft touch keys on the front of the monitor to answer.

"Are you having more troubling breathing today?"

"Are you having chest pain?"

A pleasant voice concluded with, "Thank you for completing your vital signs and remember to take your medications."

If readings were outside a person's expected measurements or a question was answered "yes," an alert was sent to the home care office where a nurse was assigned to call the patient and find out what was going on. Sometimes, for various reasons, it might be too difficult for a person to perform the monitoring session on their own, a caregiver, like Jasmine could easily do the monitoring. Miss Effie didn't necessarily need a nurse's visit every day (besides, it wasn't allowed by Medicare or Medicaid), but the agency staff would know from the readings how she was doing each day. The whole point was to catch subtle changes early. Intervene promptly. Control symptoms that could deteriorate quickly and send someone to the emergency room or hospital.

At the case conference it was decided that using a monitor would serve another purpose for Miss Effie. Given her frailty, an ambulance ride and terrifying trip to an emergency room wasn't likely to happen. The nurses agreed that a monitor would work best because they would be aware of Miss Effie's predictable decline so they could get to Miss Jasmine so she wouldn't be alone when Miss Effie passed.

There's a tangible sense of peace as we enter Miss Effie's room. She's tucked between crisp white sheets. Her withered and gnarled fingers hold the edges of a hand-stitched quilt. White downy wisps from gray cornrows rest against a pillow slip with crocheted edges.

"Slave quilt – 1863- that's what her great-great granddaughter told me," Barbara whispers.

Slipping into a narrow space between the wall and edge of the bed, Jasmine bends quietly over Miss Effie.

"Barbara brought this nice lady here. I'm gonna be able to check you every day with this here machine she has. Don't worry, she's gonna show me how it works."

I set the monitor on a waiting lace doily on the other side of the bed, plug it in, show Jasmine how it works, and take a test reading.

"Here, would you like to try on your own now? Remember, anytime you want to check Miss Effie and it's not the usual time, just push that key there. Gently now, until you hear it click and follow what the voice is saying." Jasmine nods confidently with each step.

A sound drifts in just after the monitor says, "Are you more tired today than a normal day?"

Hummm. An ever so low and lilting humming rises from the bed and continues the melody. *Swing Low Sweet Chair eee ot.*

"She hums when she's nervous or tired. It's all right Momma. It's going to be just fine."

It's time to go on to the next home. It's hard to leave. As we start retracing our steps, an unbottled perfume of humidity-kissed roses is wishing us goodbye. The humming is still with me. I wonder how long that melody had been sung, or hummed, in the fields nearby.

Back at the office several hours later Betty, the nurse watching incoming readings, meets us.

"You'll never guess what happened. We got eight transmissions from Jasmine."

I'm not understanding what she's saying. Oh no! I think. For all the hope of the technology, it didn't work! It must be the worst. Either Miss Effie had to be sent to the hospital twenty-four miles away. Or…?

"I know what you're thinking," Betty's read my mind.

"Guess what Jasmine said?"

"I just want that nice lady to know how good I could do it."

Phew! I'm relieved. They'd still have time together.

Two years later I received a Christmas card from the agency. They wanted me to know Miss Effie had passed early in December, humming, on to eternal rest from under her quilt. No ambulance, no emergency room, no hospital. Jasmine at the bedside.

There had been no need to put whispers into action again. By the holidays Jasmine had moved to Jackson to live with her stepsister and family. She took the quilt with her. A great-great-great grandchild was due in the spring who would snuggle in Jasmine's arms peeking from the beloved quilt. After that there would be a new garden to plant.

How strange I think. A patchwork quilt of feed sack scraps, printed cotton fabric and wool burlap will continue to comfort an enslaved people and their freed descendants to this very day.

I was blessed to have more home care work in Mississippi. I'm grateful for visits to homes and places where people shared their stories, their history and heritage. Mississippi stays with me as much as possible for a white girl visiting from the West who can never really understand. The following reminiscences are not about being a tourist. They give name and place to a particular homecare location that helped frame the people I met there. I can't: Order catfish without tasting Belzoni. Listen to *King's I have a Dream* without seeing Mound Bayou. Look up at a thunder cloud without spotting a tornado in a cotton field. Slap a biting mosquito without seeing a rosy sunset over the Mississippi from Rosedale observation tower. Watch a Muppets movie without recalling Kermit's birthplace near Leland.

Listen to blues on a steel guitar without being at Abe's Crossroads at Clarksdale. Smelling the perfume of roses on fences. Singing without humming.

And, pulling up my quilt on a snowy winter evening like this one.

End Note

The history African American quilts, Slave Quilts, especially linking patterns and designs to the Underground Railroad is recorded in many excellent books.

"In de winter time us'd quilt; jes go from one house to anudder in de quarter." —Martha Bradley

5 Tin Roof and Dirt Floor

You can take the guy out of the barrio, but you can't take the barrio out of the guy.
– Elizabeth Reyes

WHAT I DIDN'T WANT TO SEE was athletic shoes dangling from the overhead wire. What I did see was a carefully swept dirt yard, budding lilacs, a plank porch, and an elderly gentleman sitting in a wobbly white plastic lawn chair. Taking a frail outstretched hand and nodding my head respectfully, I say, "Buenos días, Don Jesús. ¿Cómo estás?" (Good Morning, Don Jesús, how are you?)

He stands and touches his cowboy hat brim. Sharp black eyes have visible creases at the corners from many years of squinting in the sun and smiling. He's still handsome, in his aging way at ninety- three.

"Estoy bien, gracias a Dios." (I'm fine, thank God.)

With determined steadiness, he welcomes me into a dimly lit living room placing his cane exactly as he learned from the physical therapist. I don't miss the significance of the cane or overlook the crisply ironed blue-plaid cowboy shirt and freshly laundered blue jeans-- all clues, specifically for my benefit. Six months ago, he'd fallen and broken a hip. Although the surgery to repair the fracture had been uneventful, he knew that just such things brought up this whole matter of whether he could stay here in his home any longer. More serious to him is the worry, never spoken but always present, of appearing weak to his children and grandchildren, friends, and neighbors.

"You know, being macho," say the great-grandsons the first time I met them. In Hispanic culture, whether you call it macho or not, being a man is always the highest honor and must be maintained with dignity.

"Like my grandfather there, you know. Always. Even when a *Bro* becomes a *Don*." Elbow, elbow. I get the double meaning.

It's cool inside even under a scorching sun on the tin roof. From a table, Our Lady of Guadalupe opens her starry cloak to drop roses to Juan Diego and in the flicker of a red votive candle it seems she is giving roses to Don Jesús too. And to all who enter. Walls come alive with photos of a proud family's heritage – graduations, celebrations, baptisms, birthdays, quinceaneras, weddings, a lost soldier, a returning soldier, a 70th wedding anniversary.

Doña Maria is absent, but not really. He misses her a great deal. Passed, not yet a year, into the loving care of Our Savior. She stays beside his bed in a framed wedding photo. It's a matriarchal face vibrant with youth and hope for a future. Ana, her home hospice nurse, told me about her last days and hours with the family here at her bedside. Senora's presence and strength is everywhere, a sanctuary of memorabilia inseparable from the adobe walls. Each artifact is there in its appointed place where Doña Maria last dusted it. It's still too soon to talk about her so I just touch his arm gently and let him silently remember. Recently he's begun to tell stories that match those precious life treasures so visible everywhere.

Now, and every visit, my focus is on keeping Don Jesús safe and able to stay here, until he leaves this life. This wrought iron table where we sit in the kitchen has seen many cups of coffee at dawn or afternoon visits from neighbors. Children sat here doing schoolwork, filling out college applications, crying over lost boyfriends, cradling sick babies, or worrying where the money would come from after a lost job.

I set my nursing bag on a chair seat protected by a newspaper. Reaching into an outer pocket I retrieve a quart-size Ziploc baggie with folded paper towels and a small container of liquid soap and go to the sink to wash my hands. Why does this always remind me of how difficult it was to learn about something as simple as washing your hands? Sure, it's about regulations for home visits and infection control and not taking germs from house to house. But sometimes I laugh to think about the contortions nurses go through trying to get it right. Centers for Disease Control guidelines indicate hand washing is best done at a bathroom sink, rather than a kitchen sink. As with most everything, the protocol will change based on the latest research. Just as well since the bugs are getting more resistant to our required ablutions.

Sometimes you must go for antibacterial hand sanitizer if there's no running water or various visible and invisible critters patrol and control the area. When a kitchen sink sways with stacks of unwashed dishes beside counters where uncooked meats and raw vegetables co-mingle with homeopathic remedies, reach for the hand sanitizer. Some bathroom sinks and counters are completely disguised by personal products, Lysol spray bottles, brushes and hair dryers, cosmetics and first aid supplies. So, you lather your hands with sanitizer instead, wringing your hands until they dry.

I continue a routine I can do in my sleep. Open the zipper where *the clean area* gapes open and reach a *clean* paper towel with my *clean* hands. Spread it on the table then retrieve a gallon sized Ziploc bag with blood pressure cuff, stethoscope, thermometer, and finger clip for measuring oxygen percentages. Seems like a crazy ritual. However, if you think about it, would you want to have germs from every patient the nurse has seen that day? Of course not. Every home and every visit have infection control challenges. Thank God for the invention of hand sanitizer, disinfectant wipes, and gloves, along with nurses who know when and how to use them. *What DID we do in the old days?*

"Everyone must have a way of doing their work," Don Jesús once told me while watching me set up.

I used to worry these seemingly silly requirements would embarrass or offend people. It didn't take long to realize the broader truth. It made me think differently. Consider that diabetes, heart disease, lung disease, and stroke are much more than symptoms to be kept within parameters. Each chronic condition leaves tell-tale signs and each progresses. Cancer, aging, Alzheimer's, other dementias, mental illness, catastrophic injuries eventually take over the lives of rich and poor alike. Their homes suffer too, becoming untidy and unclean, far beyond the ability of those living there to scrub and clean.

In a day's set of visits, I find suffering homes in gated communities, colonias, senior living complexes, isolated rural towns, decaying urban neighborhoods and parks of single-wide mobile homes.

Here's another important and necessary home care standard. Regulation requires every home be evaluated for safety. Is it safe enough for residents and home care staff alike? For example, is it a safety issue if a single, ungrounded extension cord sparks when it's plugged into a wall outlet? Is the outlet sprouting piggy-backed extension cords? Are lights burned out? Who would guess that puppy dogs or loving mongrels can be a fall risk? Just how much space does that pile of stuff take up? Can my patient get to the bathroom through those winding narrow pathways? What about doors? Can a person get to a door to the outside? Or to inside rooms without sending stacks careening? Where's the oxygen warning sign for both residents and visitors who are smokers?

Initially, on the first home visit, I complete a tedious, but necessary, three-page checklist. Now, thankfully, my agency has invested in mobile devices and apps to log this info. Now, each visit, I look to see if Don Jesús is following the safety precautions we've put in place. Immaculate and safe is the best way to describe what I see around me. No unwanted pests here. Hidden, but strategically placed, roach motels guard the premises. Even the dirt floor in the little sunroom, a step down from the kitchen, is sealed once a year with a special coating. Peeling linoleum has been tacked down and is scrubbed weekly. Wow, and I complain how tough I have it with my new tile floors.

Immaculate is no coincidence. Two daughters and now four granddaughters, taught by Doña Maria, have negotiated who does what when. They think nothing of it. Because of his family, Don Jesús can stay at home. And likely will die quietly in his chair on the dirt patio as he wishes. Such family bonds, especially in Hispanic and African American cultures, have existed for generations. Sometimes it makes me sad to see seniors whose adult children live in other states. Even worse, children who may live close but are often too busy to stop or stop only occasionally or maybe only on holidays.

I finish my assessment, zip my bag shut, toss the crumpled paper towel into a waste bin, wash my hands, and slip the handwashing supplies into the outside *dirty* pocket.

Luz is coming in the door. She's taken time off from work again. Thankfully it's not as often as when her great grandmother was sick and after Don Jesús came home from the hospital. She's the one who takes care of medications. This is no small matter either since there've been new and changed medications in the past two months. All have side effects that could affect his walking. This is the reason she's still visiting at the same time I'm there, whenever she can. Luz and I talk often by phone when she isn't able to be here. We go over what the doctor ordered at the last appointment; what to expect from the meds; side effects to watch for. Luz wants to be here this morning because she's noticed he's limping a little more recently from arthritic knee pain.

"I don't like taking too many pills. I don't want to get hooked on pain pills," he confesses.

They all know it was knee pain and side effects of blood pressure meds that led to that backyard fall. I listen to Luz and Don Jesús have a long exchange. A little more complicated and nuanced than my basic medical Spanish. When they finish, Luz retrieves the laundry. Don Jesus proudly shows me his pill box and identifies which ones are in which slots and what each pill is for.

"Aquí, su blanco redondo es para la presión arterial; La píldora para el dolor es esta cápsula, y esta pequeña amarilla es para el azúcar en la sangre." (Here, this round white one is for blood pressure; this capsule is for the pain, and this tiny yellow one is for blood sugar.)

He is *very* certain about what he will and will not take. He's not reluctant about taking blood pressure medicine. Prescription bottles are neatly lined up at the back of the table. A weekly pill planner box is also there. Luz takes care of re-ordering, and her son Jake picks up the refills when ready. They re-enact the weekly routine where Luz opens each bottle, reads the label and Don Jesús picks out a pill, one at a time, placing it in the correct slot. This very simple act speaks volumes. It's symbolic. Every person wants to be in control of their lives and independent, especially the elderly. Everyone receiving home care has the right to respect, dignity, and to be involved in their care, *no matter their ability*. Most of all, every one of us wants to be in our own home for as long as we live. I do. I wanted my dad to. Our lives mean something. In our homes, stories of who we are and were give us an identity.

Don Jesús' glucometer (blood sugar reader) is on the table and before I ask he tells me the numbers. He always remembers. They're dutifully recorded in a written log. If I visit before dinner, I watch him stick his finger correctly, place the blood drop on the strip and insert it into the meter. When a value is displayed, he records the number in the log. He's precise. It's a significant task that must be done correctly for him to stay independent at home. Today I check the meter's log. Right on, just as he reported. Readings have been up occasionally but what can you say about what he calls *just a little sip* of Coke or a French fry or two with his great grandson Justin. Justin has his way of contributing too. He drives by Sonic after morning classes at the community college. Although sharing forbidden foods isn't a great way to spend time with Don Jesús, it's more important that they have the time together.

"My appetite is good," Don Jesús is sure to tell me.

There was a worry he'd been losing weight recently. Sometimes his blood sugar is low. Too much coffee in the morning is the culprit.

"Sí, sometimes I'm just a little late with eating breakfast." He loves mornings listening to Tejano music from World Radio Network on a little turquoise plastic box on the windowsill. Mariachi is still his favorite. However, he does try listening to Tejano performers the grandchildren suggest.

Today he told me about his diet and eating habits.

"Ahh, but what does it hurt if my blood sugar is a little high? Sunday everyone was here for dinner. They are so so busy. Everyone works so, so hard. Mucho. They cannot babysit me every day! It's good when they are here. Tania makes tamales like Doña Maria. Refries and home-made tortillas. Good leftovers. How can one refuse?"

We always step out from the kitchen to the dirt backyard where climbing roses wind every which-way on trellises and arbors. Cherry tomato vines reach five feet.

"I have no idea how these thrive in such pitiful dirt," I remark.

"Our Lady and Doña Maria," he suggests, making the sign of the cross.

Tonight, he'll tuck himself into bed beside the wedding photo, certain to put his cane within reach, hall light on and night light on in the bathroom. Those safety tips he learned from the physical therapist are something I no longer remind him about.

He'll have already talked with Angela, his other daughter, who calls every night. Everyone is on the same page, and everyone wants the same thing. Don Jesús to be safe, independent, and happy at home.

I'm going to miss him. Soon he'll no longer qualify for Medicare intermittent skilled care. Next visit I must let him know how much longer I'll be coming and have him sign the *Advance Beneficiary Notice*. Patients have a right to know when they no longer qualify for Medicare homecare and why. In the interim I'll be talking with his doctor and reinforcing what needs to be continued to keep him healthy. I wave. He waves.

"Vaya con Dios, mi ha." (Go with God, my friend.)

6 Pigeon With A Zip Code

Pigeons go away but they always come back.

IF PIGEONS LIVED IN my post WWII suburban neighborhood in the 1950s I didn't much notice. My cousins Rick, Jim and I saw them at the city zoo on our annual summer visits. We chased them until we were hysterical and out of breath and our parents threatened never to bring us again. They told us pigeons had diseases because they lived on Skid Row with bums and sat on wires instead of tree branches. To this day I have a strange fascination with pigeons. Ever notice how pigeons always face the same direction on telephone and electrical lines?

Later, as a volunteer for a homeless clinic near Denver's old Skid Row, pigeons became daily companions. I'd visit tent shelters under old iron bridges making sure transients who came to the clinic were okay. Twenty-five years earlier the U.S. Postal Service had instituted zip codes, although being transient, pigeons and homeless people living under bridges weren't assigned a zip code, of course.

That handful of homeless camping sites under a bridge overlooked the confluence of the South Platte River and Cherry Creek in downtown Denver. In that very spot, 140 years earlier William Greeneberry "Green" Russell, newly arrived from the California gold fields, paid attention to tribal stories from his Cherokee wife about gold flakes in the riverbed. He didn't find many but did set off the Pike's Peak Gold Rush that later became the Colorado Gold Rush. Gold seekers came by the thousands to the makeshift town of Auraria. Teamsters haggling over mule prices; hucksters and suppliers peddling overpriced shovels, tents, and sluicing pans made deals behind town stables. Prospectors with a few flakes from a lucky spot elsewhere could wrangle a sleeping spot on the floor of a nearby clapboard hotel, alongside a dozen snoring drunks.

Everywhere I traveled bridges and rivers were often part of the landscape. And every city had its share of pigeons. On a drab dreary February day in 1999 I met a very lucky pigeon living in Brooklyn zip code 11204.

Each morning, I look from my eighth-floor window at the Brooklyn Marriott into a subdued winter sunrise to where the Twin Towers overshadow Wall Street. Everybody's in a big hurry down at street level. Pedestrians and bicyclists are streaming across Brooklyn Bridge to work in Manhattan. Half asleep, I stare at the seemingly fathomless East River. At the center of a chaotic intersection, a no-nonsense policewoman is fearlessly directing foot, auto, and bridge traffic. Clearly, she's in charge.

Eddie, the Dunkin' Donut guy, is waiting for me and smiles as the hotel's revolving door spits me out onto the sidewalk. A decaf with cream and a bag of two raised glazed are waiting at the end of his arm.

"Here ya go. Lookin' good, lookin' good. Let's be careful out there."

Coffee steam fogs my glasses. I can barely make out the pathetic little tree in the street median. A single leaf dangles precariously from a twisted branch. Its growth is stunted by carbon dioxide, no sun, and dog pee. It's become a friend. Many years later I read the classic book *A Tree Grows in Brooklyn*.

I miss my Rocky Mountain home of snow-covered evergreens. I'm sorry, Maya Angelou. Sometimes I'm just not good at listening to your advice:

"I long, as every human being, to be at home wherever I find myself."

I just can't be at home here.

Most days I drive. Some days I'm chauffeured into dangerous neighborhoods. Either the driver or the building security guard rides up the elevator with me to make sure I exit at the floor I'm supposed to and haven't disappeared. I've never experienced such richness of humanity from so many cultures in so many different neighborhoods. It's as if Lady Liberty personally escorted the huddled masses to this place.

In every home, the memories of life events and family traditions are tucked away in aging minds. As I visit, just the mention of places retrieves details of yesteryears. The only thing that troubles me is not enough time to listen to all the stories. I visit Sephardic Jewish patients and their families before sundown on Friday and Eastern Rite Catholic Russian immigrants who attend St. Nicholas Ukrainian Church on Sunday in Park Slope. I'm deeply pained and forever humbled by listening to Holocaust survivors and hide my tears knowing I can never make up for the horrors. New immigrants from Ukraine have that flush of determination and energy to build new lives in a new land. I laugh at Irish blarney and learn the meaning of craic.

At each home, personal stories are longing to be told. With delight the person comes alive for *that nice nurse*.

"I've lived here all my life."

"Grew up in East Flatbush, off Utica."

"Those were the days. Me and my Dad went to Ebbets Field every Saturday when the Dodgers played. By golly, that was baseball at its best. Now that Gil Hodges was the best first baseman ever, I say. Jackie Robinson said so too."

"Ya know, it was mighty tough during the Depression. My brother and me hung out at Wallabout collecting junk to sell. We lost him in the war."

"My Bubbeh cried when Frankel's delicatessen at the Navy Yard closed. Let's see, that was back in '47."

"I had my first drink at McSorley's Old Ale House. Grampa Charlie took me."

"See that old fiddle on the wall over there? Played a lot a jigs and reels I did. Ballads too. Saturday night ceilis (Irish gatherings.) The whole family went. My sister danced. My grandpa recited poems."

"We walked every Sunday to the Botanic Garden."

"I can still taste ice cream from the Good Humor Man. It was sure swell on a hot August afternoon."

I'll share my secret – I've developed a fascination with names of neighborhoods, streets, and places. I collect them in little notebooks as souvenirs. Myrtle, Flatbush, Flushing, Furman, Jay. Farragut Road, BQE, Prospectus Expressway. Cobble Hill, Vinegar Hill, Greenwood Heights, Red Hook, Sheepshead Bay, Brooklyn Heights, Parkville, Bushwick, Cobble Gardens, Gowanus. Here various parkways spider east leading to neighborhoods that border parks or face expressways. Do any readers recognize the names?

I'm fascinated by the styles of old buildings too. Neighborhoods are nothing like our western suburban neighborhoods, filled with one-story ranch homes. Most curious to me are three-story brownstones where three or more families live. One day I'm visiting five-story wooden apartments surrounded by barbed wire and sprouting TV antennas among drying laundry. Another day I enter the retirement village of Seagate where I feel like I'm stepping on holy ground. Secluded and protected, this is the last dwelling place of survivors of genocide. Their small cinder block ranch homes, painted a glowing white, face the Atlantic at Norton Point. A new Jerusalem? I've walked to Seagate from Coney Island's parking lot. One day, I finish at Brighton Beach where eastern European families rejoice at escape from Russian oppression.

Today, on a certain street, in a certain neighborhood, I meet a pigeon living on the third floor of a brownstone.

To set the scene, I'm reminded of the 1987 movie *Batteries Not Included* with famous actors Jessica Tandy and Hume Cronyn. Faye and Fred Riley own a neighborhood diner, Fred's the cook, Faye's the waitress. She's happy in a state of perpetual Alzheimer's waiting for Bobby, their only child, to come home. She doesn't remember the car crash that killed him. They live above their café in an apartment building that has been condemned and is scheduled for demolition. It's a tender magical story. Today, instead of alien mechanical life-forms that save the residents in the movie, the residents I'm visiting in this brownstone save another type of aerial life form.

Stepping into the brownstone's entryway is like stepping into the movie. I look down and see hundreds of hexagonal white ceramic tiles. Above my head hangs a massive Tiffany chandelier on a chain anchored in the ceiling four floors up. Eight brass mailboxes line the left wall. I start up a five-foot wide oak staircase, sure to be the original, to the first-floor landing with two apartments, one left the other right. Leaded stained-glass transoms above each door are open. Classical composer Giuseppe Verdi's opera Aida, a tragic love story, fills the first-floor landing. Across from 101, a Chopin nocturne on a 33 rpm vinyl record plays on a portable turntable.

I pause briefly and close my eyes to listen to the nocturne. On the second-floor landing lyrics from the metal band Public Enemy throbs from a boom box in 201. Across the landing the cast of Days of Our Lives acts out yet another year of tragedies in the city of Salem on a black and white TV screen I can see through the slightly open door. It's a different matter at the third-floor landing. A disturbing non-food aroma emanates from 302. I look for a fire extinguisher. None. I hunt for a fire escape. None, silly me. Fire escapes are connected to apartment windows and lead down wrought iron stairways to a telescoping ladder that drops to the ground. I knock at 301. A dead bolt is unlocked. A chain slides. A door opens.

"Hey there, did you find it OK? Oh yeah, I'm Vicki."

"I'm glad today worked for you and your mom," I reply. Then I repeat the explanation I gave on the phone of why I'm visiting.

"Can we sit at the table? Sometimes it's easier to go over medications there."

She leads me to a round table with a red-checkered plastic tablecloth that looks like it belongs in the Italian restaurant at street level. Instead of a shaker of Parmesan cheese, a dozen or more pill bottles take up space. I overlook a stainless-steel bowl of water in the center of the table. As I'm about to sit in one of the three chairs, a flapping of wings ruffles the hair on the top of my head. I stare. What just happened? Surely that's not a pigeon I see drinking out of the bowl.

"Oh, don't mind Poor Dear. We were sure he was dead when we found him on the outside window ledge."

"He just laid there like this."

She bends over the table, flops her head down and rolls her eyes back to demonstrate what a limp pigeon looks like. Poor Dear dropped from the sky almost a month ago which is not uncommon in Brooklyn, or anywhere else in the greater NYC area. Apparently, he was knocked limp and goofy, or dead, by who knows what. Most often birds veer off course and slam into a window too hard. Vicki continues.

Next day Mom says, "Vicki, why are you putting breadcrumbs by his beak? He'll never make it."

"Ya just never know," continues Vicki.

In all my times visiting under the bridge inhabited by pigeons, I never learned to determine if a pigeon was male or female. And I don't want to know now. But I do know what pigeon nesting places look like. Poor Dear's nest is situated inside the transom. Miniature bits of stuffing from the couch and a few tangles of hair, plucked, I suspect from a hairbrush, are hidden among sticks and leaves. It's a bit unusual. What else is the matter? Uh, the nest is on the wrong side. It should be on the hallway side. No, that's not right. It shouldn't be inside the building at all. How did he get all those twigs and sticks in? Droppings down the door frame confirm it's true. He's settled in.

"Vicki, do you always keep the water bowl on the table?"

"Sure do."

"Even during meals?

"Uh huh."

"And you take your medicines here at the table?"

"Every day like clockwork."

Poor Dear pecks on the lids of med bottles.

"Shoo, shoo." I wave my arm and thankfully Poor Dear flies to a sunny spot on the bay windowsill.

Standing up and going to the sink to wash my hands, I opt to use sanitizer. A chipped porcelain sink is piled and overflowing with dirty dishes. I'm sure my 20-ounce bottle of sanitizer will be used up by the end of the visit. Stepping back to the table, I proceed to set up the familiar clean area, It turns out there isn't enough space to lay out everything – blood pressure cuff, stethoscope, thermometer. This visit is becoming even more complicated.

"Okay," I say to myself, "… adapt, get creative. This is going to be a little tricky." I try to ignore the pigeon feathers on the table. I'm sure Vicki sees me wince.

At that point, Vicki's mom joins us. She's been asleep on a roll-away bed in the living room. There's no bedroom so it's called a buffet apartment. Vicki sleeps on the couch. Mom makes certain I know how devoted Vicki is to caring for Poor Dear.

"Oh, isn't it wonderful? When he landed on the windowsill, he only had a few feathers and was just a skinny little set of bones. Maybe it was the aspirin I mixed in water and fed him. The dropper from my eye drops worked perfectly. Now, look at him! Those shiny gray feathers. I suppose we're going to have to let him go sooner or later."

I keep reminding myself I'm not her home healthcare nurse. The only reason I'm here is to gather data for a university study on how home healthcare nurses make decisions. This woman's primary nurse surely has a challenge on her hands.

"Tell me about how you get groceries Vicki," I ask, stepping to open the refrigerator. "May I?"

It's so empty my voice echoes when I peer in to discover an opened quart of milk, a pack of Mountain Dew, and a pizza box with three wrinkled slices. I suspect this refrigerator hasn't seen fresh vegetables for quite some time.

"I noticed a market on the corner. Do you shop there?"

"You bet. Everybody in the neighborhood goes there. Mr. Janssen still works three days a week even though his son Joe and daughter-in-law Maggie have taken over. I went to school with Joe."

"What kind of groceries can you get there?"

"Pretty much anything you want." Vicki holds up the half bag of Fritos.

The only corner markets I know from home are 7-Elevens specializing in chips, pork rinds, cookies, soda, bologna, and hot dogs grilled between a set of mechanical rollers until they're almost ash. New York corner markets are ubiquitous and reflect the rich culture of the ethnic neighborhoods where they're located. Sometimes on the way home to the Marriott I buy fresh fruit and vegetables to eat for dinner. Warm crusty bread, specialty cheese. Genoa salami and olives. Mediterranean figs. I fill my hotel room's ice bucket with water for a bouquet of fresh flowers. Of the many sights I've seen while in New York, it's those buckets of fresh flowers that sit out front of the markets that always make me smile.

A package of Hostess Cupcakes and hot dog buns lie on the counter. Crumbs leave a trail to the windowsill. Poor Dear's dinner with dessert?

"He likes those buns better than bread. Especially if I leave them out so they're a little bit crusty."

I sneak a quick glance at the linoleum for ants or roaches that are hiding in dark places during the day. It never ceases to amaze me how people are just trying to live. All of us really. To have a place of our own, something to eat, people or pets that bring a little happiness into our lives. I often wonder if Vicki ever set Poor Dear free.

End Note

West Nile Virus - Bird Flu - 1999

West Nile Virus, or bird flu, was isolated in 1937 in a resident living in the West Nile district of Northeastern Uganda. Outbreaks became more widespread in Africa by the 1970s. The summer of 1999 was the first time this Old-World virus had been identified in America, presenting with a cluster of severe cases of encephalitis (inflammation of the brain) in and around Queens, just across the East River from Brooklyn. At the same time a high rate of bird fatalities was noted in and around NYC. Birds of all species dwindled, especially crows. And pigeons. West Nile virus infections in humans continued to be reported throughout the country.

In 2003, the virus was identified on the front range of the Rocky Mountains where a newly identified mosquito carrier was discovered, and my home state of Colorado, like many other states began implementing widespread insecticide spraying. I wonder if the homeless people under the bridge over the Platte River got sprayed.

Emergency room staff and doctor's offices were always the first to see symptoms. Cases ranged from mild to those requiring hospitalization, and seven people died here in Colorado. Symptoms could last for months. Consequently, home healthcare nurses and physical therapists were needed, post hospitalization, to manage recovery at home.

As the numbers of infectious diseases increased, global

health monitoring by the World Health Organization grew. Autoimmune Deficiency Syndrome - 1987 (AIDS); Avian flu/ West Nile Virus - 1990s followed by H1N1/swine flu epidemic -2009; Ebola in 2014, and Zika in 2016. In January 2020, a new strain of the SARS virus, coronavirus, was declared a pandemic in China, where it originated. Travel bans were put into effect across the globe and mandatory quarantines were established at international ports. The World Health Organization again mobilized strategies and actions based on lessons learned and strategies applied. However, approximately 80% of the world's population was restricted to homes beginning in March 2020, nicely called *Shelter in Place*. All non-essential businesses were closed. By the end of 2020 almost a million people died in the U.S. Memories of victims were honored on the Washington Mall on inauguration day 2021 with 900,000 American flags and burning candles. Deaths finally peaked at over 1 million. Yet, variants continue. The world is not the same and never will be.

I've been exposed to and escaped H1N1, Eboli, AIDS, streptococcus infections that injure heart valves; blood borne pathogens, tick bites that cause encephalitis (brain inflammation) C-diff diarrhea, MRSA (Methicillin Resistant Staphylococcus Aureus), SARs outbreaks, and all the various strains of flu and cold viruses. My working years spanned the days before Theraflu, Tamiflu, and Airborne. Back in the day I was traveling, cold and flu viruses were treated with plenty of orange juice, Vitamin C, chicken soup and rest. Who knows why I never developed West Nile virus in 1999 when once upon a time I met a pigeon in Brooklyn.

Viruses have had major influences on the genesis and evolution of life.
Viruses are embedded into the very fabric of life.
– Luis P. Villarreal
Evolutional Scientist; Professor Emeritus,
University of California-Irvine.

7 Chicks, Ticks and Grasshoppers

A grasshopper is nothing,
but a mosquito turned hulk.......

VALLEY VIEW HOME CARE had been certified to provide skilled home health services since the late 1980s and won several home care awards over the years. The previous year the agency's management decided to become nationally accredited and chose our organization. Accreditation is a major undertaking, and they wisely took a year preparing for the onsite survey. Onsite surveys are always unannounced, although once the agency turns in a self-evaluation and payment a surveyor is guaranteed to arrive within 60-90 days. I wasn't surprised when I arrived and handed the receptionist my business card. She stares at me and stammers.

"You're really from there?"

I've had a variety of responses. Numerous doors shut in my face. Receptionists who faint, staff who disappear and administrators who argue they aren't ready yet; come another time.

We began the three-day onsite visit with an Opening Conference as usual. It was encouraging to see that the day's visit schedule was rearranged so that all staff could attend. That's a signal everyone was committed and part of the preparation. Employees even came in on their day off. On the first day of a survey, I select five patients we'll visit the next day.

At this time there was a national phenomenon affecting agencies nationwide. With the onset of managed care, hospital patients were being discharged sooner and were much sicker when they returned home. As a result nurses needed to spend extra time in the home for these patients.

Home visit day was a typical July day in Restonville. By 8 a.m. the heat index is hovering at 100 and climbing. Gloria is the nurse I'll be with for the day. Staff come and go replenishing car coolers with extra water bottles for patients and a second cooler for lunches and snacks. One of our patients needs blood drawn so there will be a specific ice pack cooler for the blood vials. This gives me an opportunity to see how Gloria organizes supplies in the car. And, how she protects the confidentiality of files she carries in the car.

Gloria says, "The first visit will take at least forty minutes to get to the house. Valley View has patients located both in town and over a wide territory of rural or semi-rural homes reached by a network of paved and dirt roads. Once we leave a paved road at the end of town, we take a long winding dirt road."

"You can go out to the car if you like. It's the maroon Mazda. I have the air conditioning going."

"OK."

As I open the door I'm pinned between the door and screen by a yellow-green grasshopper staring down at me with iridescent compound eyes. He's a whopper hopper the size of a small helicopter. He is irreverently called *gawd awful creature*. I scream and everyone runs to the door.

"Oh, I was just startled," I say nonchalantly. "No worries. I have a long not-so-pleasant relationship with grasshoppers. Besides it's impossible to describe the sick panicky feeling grasshoppers give me. I've walked more than a block to avoid going past a grasshopper on the sidewalk."

At first, we chatted about the weather and news I saw on the local TV station while having breakfast. I remark about the July 4th celebrations and the little league baseball team.

"Gloria, can I ask you a few questions on our drive? It helps me understand the agency's various care processes?"

"Sure, but first I have a question for you. Did you ever have a patient caseload?"

I laugh. It's an unusual question. There's a circulating myth that surveyors haven't taken care of patients directly.

"That's a fair question. Yes, for about ten years. Sometimes I miss having patients of my own. In a way, though, I almost do have a caseload because I visit different homes now with agency nurses. I always learn something from them. It's also a way to keep up with trends and practices."

"Tell me a little about yourself, Gloria."

Before we both knew it she told me a lot about herself. She worked as an aide at the local nursing home when she was in high school. Because of her keen interest and strong skills, she was encouraged by the evening shift RN to become a Licensed Practical Nurse (LPN). When she graduated, Valley View was hiring LPNs. That was the year she and Steve were married and the increase in her hourly wage helped with the budget and starting a family. As most of us have, she was smitten with home care visits to townsfolk she'd known all her life. When her kids, Rachel and Dan, went to school she started working full-time. Across the country increased demand for more nurses resulted in local community colleges establishing an RN to BSN (Bachelor of Science Nursing) program. Both day and evening classes were scheduled so students could work part time. Gloria had graduated this past Spring. It wasn't easy managing a household, working part-time, studying, and writing papers. There had often been a scramble at home for computer time. She had just told me the common story of home care nurses in smaller rural areas and towns like Restonville who continued their education from nurse aide to LPN to BSN through Community College outreach programs.

"Gloria, you must be so proud of all you've accomplished."

"I couldn't have done it without the RNs at Valley View.

Sandra, my supervisor rearranged my schedule to accommodate classes. My friend Karen picked up Rachel and Dan from school and took them home to her house for dinner on nights I had class."

"Now, how about your patient Jean who we're headed to see?"

"It's a sad story. Jean took over the commercial chicken farming business a few years ago when her husband Ray died of stomach cancer. Ray's great grandfather started farming on this land in 1879. Jean and her son Ray Jr. and a family cousin each own a third of the business. Ray Jr. manages the transport-to-market side of the business, driving one and overseeing three other eighteen wheelers."

"Every year when allergy season hits Jean's asthma kicks up. She continues to smoke. But what can I say? Tobacco is her addiction. You name it, she's got it. Obesity, COPD (Chronic Obstructive Pulmonary Disease,) hypertension, adult-onset diabetes. She's just come home from a week at Beverly's rehab unit after a hospitalization. She has so many new and changed medications and no idea what to take when. Fretting and worrying about money and paying bills keeps her in a stew most of the time. This summer made everything worse between the humidity and her general poor health and debilitation.

"The house is a perpetual disaster since she took on the books and started driving a school bus to make ends meet. Sometimes life just isn't fair to some people, is it? It seems to chew them up and spit them out.

"With Jean, I sense she has never reconciled how much her life changed after Ray died. She'll never be able to do what she used to. She was an immaculate housekeeper to the point of what we would now consider obsessive-compulsive. She barely gets around in a wheelchair without footrests, propelled by using her feet. She spends the day going from room to room organizing piles of stuff to have a garage sale, give to friends, or send to the Salvation Army thrift store."

I can't help but say, "Isn't that what all of us go through as we get older? We think we're the same person we used to be."

Gloria continues, "Jean's nephew Jack moved in two months ago and is now her primary caregiver. He's still unemployed. Work is hard to come by around here. It gives them all day to quibble about what's good for her, or not. He means well. So, that's her story."

There's a pause. We turned onto another dirt road, and I look up from writing notes. I'm speechless. Wire fences and wooden posts are glowing iridescent lime green and lemon yellow in the blazing sun. Hundreds, no, thousands of grasshoppers, are sunning, stacked in two and three layers.

As we pull into the driveway and around the backdoor Jim Boy, a much-loved loppy eared hound dog, looks up from a shady spot and moseys our way to say hello. Gloria parks as close to the back door as possible so we can hustle from car to house. Gloria called Jack last night to let him know we were coming around ten. He's watching for us.

"Let's gather our bags and make a run for it," she suggests.

Just as I open the car door the greenest and biggest gawd awful lands smack dab in the middle of my forehead and my eyes cross. Next, one lights on my forearm with a thwack of its prehensile crispy legs. A third one selects the back of my neck. I'm afraid to move but more than that the worst nausea is making me gag.

"What's that sickening smell!?"

"Hurry, here grab my arm. Run to the back porch and step up into the kitchen."

We stumble into a damp darkness. Sheets have been tacked over the windows. Two box fans are sitting silent. Jean is yelling and short of breath.

"We got a problem here Gloria! A real problem, a REALLY BIG problem! The power has been out since four this morning. I tried to call you a little while ago. Rural electric promised to come out soon. That was four hours ago! Jack covered the windows. It was the only thing we could think of to keep out the sun and try to stay cool in the kitchen and wait. Overlook the mess," she apologizes.

"Jean, can we just get the visit done? This is the surveyor that I told you about." I quickly explain my purpose and take a place at the back of the table. Jean is clearly distracted. Gloria is listening to Jean's lung sounds.

"I hear crackles, gurgles, and pops because the airways are reacting to the stress and your blood pressure is up. Have you used your nebulizer?"

Gloria rolls her eyes. I'm sure she's thinking *that's a silly question*. No electricity to run it.

"Have you been using your oxygen?"

"Yeah, just two liters awhile this morning. I called the delivery guy to see if he could bring me an extra backup tank since the concentrator is on low reserve now," Jean is going on and on. "Oh God, I just can't think straight, I'm so worried. Smoked almost a pack already! I was doing soooo good about cutting back."

She is chattering a mile a minute as Jack, and I help her stand on the scale. Gloria is worried that Jean may pick up extra water weight in her feet and ankles, making it even more difficult to get around. She's pushing 205 lbs.

"How's it going with the diet and meal plan we worked on last week?"

Jack pipes up, "I keep telling her she just can't be eatin' this kind of stuff. I heard on Dr. Oz all about those sweets and putting on all that weight. I've been reading on the web too about this diabetes. Lot of people have suggestions about what to do."

"I'll eat what I damn well please."

"No, you won't. I'll cook what I think you're supposed to eat," he says standing with his arms folded and face screwed up in a frown. This is an example of the complicated patients Gloria and the other nurses visit. Jean is one of many; some more sick than others.

Jean's CB radio is crackling with broadcasts. Today is a full delivery day for Ray Jr. and the three other semi drivers who are on the road. On a usual day they load and leave before 6 a.m. to deliver to two plants. One plant processes fryers. One processes layers. It's a 100-mile round trip for each.

"Ten-four Rooster 3. Watch for detours around Marysville. Tyson's emergency location is opening."

"Roger, Duke 2. Power out in four counties."

"Copy that. Chester 1 here. Power back on down south of Highway 40."

"Copy that, Ray 2. Truck unloaded at Plant 5 hours of emergency backup there."

Jean sucks in a breath of relief and the rosary she was praying drops on the table leaving dents on her fingers. Ray will be home in an hour. Gloria shares her relief and gives her a big hug.

"Jean, I'm so glad he'll be home soon. We'll be taking off now. When we get to a cell tower, I'll call Gerry at the office. She'll check in with Rural Electric to make sure you're on the emergency assistance list in case the power doesn't come back on soon. Try to call me or leave a message at the office anytime. I'll call you this afternoon when I can."

"Oh, Gloria. We'll lose everything! Everything!"

Gloria and I dash to the car. Thank goodness for Jim Boy who gets up from under a willow tree and lopes out to the car with us like a bodyguard. Where did those evil menaces retreat to?

"Gloria, tell me more about why Jean is so panicked."

"See those three warehouses over the hill there? Each of those buildings houses 30,000 chickens and more than two dozen ventilation fans. Listen. That's the sound of massive backup generators in each building that are now powering ventilation fans. They're good for ten hours max. That's 2 o'clock. It's impossible to predict how many chickens they could possibly lose even if the electricity does come back on. The business would go bankrupt, leading to foreclosure on the farm and business. And that disgusting smell? It's normal. In counties where commercial chicken production is the local economy there's no escaping it. You get used to it and hardly notice it."

What a long hot day we had. Farm to farm where fields and fences remain bright yellow. The electricity came back on just thirty minutes after we left.

I spent the final day in the office completing Valley View's survey report. Everyone participated in the preparations and worked hard to put into place decidedly tough standards and every employee deserved to be complimented. The entire staff attended the Exit Conference. There was every reason to celebrate. I witnessed excellent nursing care in homes and documentation that accurately reflected what happened to each patient.

Jean and Ray lost fewer than a hundred chickens. As I was leaving, Gloria noticed a Band-Aid covering the quarter-size red welt on my right calf.

"Is that OK? What happened?"

"Oh, just where I had to remove a tick. Guess old Jim Boy got a little too close trying to protect me from the grasshoppers!"

8 So, You're Black

Simply put, stories help you learn to empathize with other people as you come to understand their point of view.
—Unknown

Have you ever asked yourself *who am I and where did I come from*? It's a question that sooner or later wiggles its way into our human minds demanding answers. You know. Some time or another we ask *THE QUESTION.*

"Daddy, how did I get here? Was I adopted? I don't look like my sister and brother."

Family holiday gatherings provoke questions of ancestry. Remember that aunt who came to Thanksgiving dinner and you hid under the table so she wouldn't squeeze you to death? The Uncle who smelled like beer and told fishing stories? *Oooh Gross! Are they really part of my family?*

Shoe boxes of photos were brought out of the closet. Photos of great-great grandparents balancing babies in front of sod homesteads, street cars and trolleys. Camping trips. Afternoons at the beach. Summer vacations in National Parks, skiing at Aspen, canoeing in the Adirondacks, geysers at Yellowstone, Magic Mountain at Disneyland. Some of us were expected to sit quietly on the couch to watch home movies. A little girl doing cartwheels on a lawn. A toddler squealing over two candles on a birthday cake and squeezing frosting between chubby fingers. A son in a Boy Scout uniform. A junior angler's first trout catch.

That's how my generation learned who we were and where we came from. An American narrative of typical white history where people and places had names. Full names. Given names and middle names linked to ancestors. Ancestors with an identifiable legacy. For the most part. Names after somebody. These days scrapbooks of newspaper clippings and photos are being dusted off by grandmothers who were young activists in the Civil Rights Movement of the 1960s.

Not all Americans have such a tidy history of who they are and where they came from. During the transatlantic slave trade twelve million Africans were forced onto ships. Slave ship manifests from the 1700s list only the names of the ships and their captains, number of slaves, and departing and arriving ports. Who were these human beings with only numbers for names? What became of them after they came ashore in America? Storyteller and diver Tara Roberts and fellow African American divers are using their skills to tell an inclusive story of the slave trade. They're uncovering the stories buried underwater.

"Being connected with your ancestors is a very powerful thing. If you break your connectivity, it's like you're wandering around lost."

On Tuesday nights I eat dinner in front of the TV as Dr. Henry Louis Gates Jr. searches for more history in his weekly PBS TV program *Finding Your Roots*. He has spent a lifetime and career in recovering the stories. In the wake of George Floyd's murder in Detroit in 2020 a new generation of African Americans is exploring who they are, where they came from and where they're going. *Kamau Sadiki – Divers with a purpose. (DWP)* are part of putting the scrapbook together. I'm drawn back to the year I was making home visits with nurses in Virginia.

"So, you're black," states Quentin the RN I'm accompanying.

"Yes, son, I am," replies Miss Esther with pride.

Her rocking continues like a metronome. Tic Toc, Tic Toc, back forth, back forth. She smiles at me as I try to sit inconspicuously in a side chair. Four adult daughters are planted on the couch behind her. One is clearly unhappy, one is trying to stifle a laugh, one rolls her eyes and mouths "What the hell?!!"

Daughter number four stands up and makes a break for the bathroom. They've all convened to oversee and supervise this first home care visit to their mother. Quentin is a tall handsome recent graduate RN. Enthusiasm and eagerness surround his serious and professional intentions. He's balancing a clipboard on his lap. He looks up sheepishly, embarrassed. He's black too.

I'm here on behalf of a University Research Center noted for its long history in studying the growth and development of nursing homes and home health care. For over a year now, home care nurses have been conducting a federally mandated assessment of each adult patient they admit. OASIS, the document the nurse is to fill out, was NOT well received. I'm public enemy Number One. After a year of implementation, I'm returning to agencies to verify that OASIS is being correctly implemented. OASIS caused a lot of protests and backlash. Unfortunately, agencies created assessment documents that were unnecessarily too long. I'm in Virginia making joint visits with patients' nurses. I quietly observe how the clinician completes the assessment. Then I record my own findings. This isn't the most comfortable start.

I politely but nervously look over at Quentin who is happily proceeding to *gather data*. To him, like many of his peers, OASIS is just a checklist. As if he'll get a dollar for every box checked. I 've heard that some agencies are paying an extra twenty-five dollars per visit. I've introduced myself and my purpose to Miss Esther, age eighty-nine, and her daughters who have taken off work to attend the visit. Miss Esther has a twinkle in her eyes and is patiently responding to his inquiries – interrogation is a better word.

"You can get off and, on the toilet, and take a shower, right?"

"Oh yes, just fine, son," she nods confidently.

The sisters all shake their heads no.

I cringe again as Couch Four weighs in with the same cringe as mine, although for different reasons. I fantasize they will start holding up BOO! signs. They know she can't do those activities. I know that OASIS was never intended to be a questionnaire. To get accurate and useful information about what Miss Esther really needs is to perform an integrated comprehensive assessment – a term originating because of the implementation of OASIS.

"Will you be my nurse, young man?"

"Yes, Miss Esther it's an honor."

"Thas good, uh- hum, thas good," and on she rocks.

Quentin was just as relieved as I was to be leaving. I wanted to apologize to the daughters, but that's not right. This is a community that's proud of its young adult professionals. Together back at the office I demonstrate how a comprehensive assessment is done.

"Quentin, try this."

"Let me help you up Miss Esther and we'll walk to the bathroom, and you can show me how you manage taking a bath and using the toilet." Using the integrated assessment approach, he and I go through every data item, from using a walker to taking medications.

"I did everything wrong didn't I?" he worries.

"Not exactly. You meant well. The most important thing to remember as a home care nurse is that your patients are people, not numbers. Not defined by a Medicare number, or a set of data points to be tallied. Not just symptoms to be care-planned for. Ask, then listen to what they say, and don't say. Observe every little thing. Clues to their past and present are all around. Ask important questions that don't result in misjudgment. Don't ask *Can you or do you*. Instead ask *tell me how you*. Have them describe how their day goes. In the beginning I didn't have these comprehensive assessment skills either. It's takes time."

"Be kind to yourself. Did you see how Miss Esther looked at you?

She was beaming. She could never have imagined, in her

lifetime, being visited in her home by a nurse, a black nurse who's a man."

Listen to her. Listen to her stories from a time in history when black men and women didn't have a history of their own. What history they had was written by white men."

I had the next day off so decided to visit a special exhibit on slavery at the National Picture Gallery in Washington D.C. I wasn't prepared. A single shocking vintage photo hangs alone in the middle of a white wall causing me to sit down on the bench below the photo. Tears are dripping down to my clenched hands as my nose drips. I feel like I've been punched in the gut. In the photo a dozen black men are dangling from a tree. Somebody's son, father, husband, brother, nephew, grandson. A security guard is closing the building for the day.

"Oh my God, I say to him sniffling. I get it, I really get it." He sits down beside me, puts his arm around me and hands me a Kleenex.

"It's okay, take as long as you need. It's our history. It's where we've come from."

Names of modern victims of brutality create news flashes, clog social media, and fill courtrooms. Truths of an ignominious past are unearthed. At the same time a proud and rich history is being documented by Black artists, musicians, poets, physicists, astronauts, educators, historians, social workers, and lawyers and divers, to mention only a few. In a not so distant past their ancestors had no history at all, no knowledge of who they were. Historians are now accurately describing the events of the past for the first time. Miss Esther and Quentin are bookends to a too long ignored story.

9 Pest Control

I'm convinced my cockroaches have military training,
I set off a roach bomb – they diffuse it.
—Jay London

G'DAY MATE!

We welcomed Geico Gecko into our TV homes in 2000. He's become our little green pal who will at least wish us a happy day in his Aussie brogue when no one else does. He's captured our hearts. I kind of like the idea of a little lizard that has my back. A cement mixer could demolish my car and he'd make it all better while patting me on the back. During the pandemic I wished Martin (that's his real name) could sit on the couch and have a chat to cheer me up. Martin, America's most loved reptile, has a nemesis. The American cockroach.

911 – Elberts scrolls across the digital screen on my beeper. I'm already on my way. Dalene meets me at the door. She gives me *the look*. I know what this is about.

"I ain't never seen the likes of these! I'm tellin' you I'm done this time! I'm never comin' back. This is the last time I'm going chase these monsters around the bathtub watchin' Mr. Elbert come to his end."

Cockroaches may be one of the worst environmental concerns that home care staff encounter. These notorious insect criminals break and enter through small cracks in walls, gaps in electric sockets and switch plates, and up through drains near food sources. As the saying goes, *they'll eat you out of house and home* by feasting on food scraps, aluminum cans, book covers and pages, newspapers, and even human hair.

By her look she's downright mad. I don't blame her.

"I'll clean the tub, Dalene, go ahead and change the sheets." I patted her back trying to calm her down.

Roaches are so thick in the antique clawfoot bathtub I can imagine the beasts picking it up and walking it down the hall. A few who've apparently gotten their drink are moving on to the kitchen. It's the worst roach invasion I've seen. Something must be done. Mr. Elbert's lungs won't hang on much longer. After fifty years the effects of being exposed to asbestos while working in Navy shipyards during WWII, has taken a toll. Air sacs in the lungs have thickened and become dysfunctional. He jokes about his tail, fifty feet of oxygen tubing connected to an oxygen concentrator. He's made up a little jingle: *"Give me air, Give me air. Or else I can't go anywhere."*

The effects are inescapable: High blood pressure, severe difficulty breathing, fatigue and obesity. Diabetes. To complicate matters Jim and Mae live on the second floor of a historic brick two story called a Denver box.

Back at the office we put our heads together. What are the options, if any? Professional exterminators? Aren't they toxic and dangerous? I call George, Mr. Elbert's son.

"I'll look into it," he promises. The next day he called back. "Not good news. Adams Pest Control offered discount pricing, but the amount and type of pesticides needed require Mom and Dad be out of the building for two weeks. Can't see that happening, can you?"

Next day we bivouac at Elbert's.

"What about geckoes?" interrupts eleven-year-old Jimmy as we sit at the Elbert's kitchen table.

Tanisha, his mom, says, "What? That sounds crazy."

A dozen roaches bolt from the sink drain when Jimmy turns an overhead light on.

"No wait, wait – we've been studying them in Mr. Wilson's science class. Geckoes eat lizards." He's completely serious.

"No way. Uh huh, yes they do."

"How many are in those walls? How many can one gecko eat.?" I wonder.

By the time I left the visit a plan had been hatched and the troops called in. Roach Day is set. A going away party for roaches, compliments of *Ghostbuster Geckos*. One week family and church and neighborhood volunteers scour the house from top to bottom with safe odorless non-toxic cleaners. Cupboards and closets are inspected thoroughly and wiped down with vinegar. Every potential roach breach location is identified and tagged with blue tape. Jim watches the World Series in his bedroom that has been stripped bare except for the Brooklyn Dodgers game ball from 1946. New trash cans with lids are donated. Plumbers Local Union #3 donates and installs a new walk-in/roller chair shower with a wide bath bench. The old claw foot tub is carried downstairs to the front yard and planted with flowers. Dalene and I high-five. Jim reads his Marvel comics in preparation for donating to the Boys & Girls Clubs. Jimmy and his buddies gather and dispose of newspapers and magazines. They shelve books that had been lying on the floor. Saturday the next week Dave Wilson, Jimmy's science teacher, drives fifty miles to Colorado Springs to collect six donated geckos from an exotic pet store.

"Hey, man, just let me know if you need help. That's really cool what you're doing." Jerry the lizard guy slaps him on the back.

Dave arrived at the gathering of volunteers with a total of eighteen geckos: twelve from local pet shops. Scrub buckets, brooms and vacuums appeared in the entryway and a final clean preceded *the launch*. A total of nine roach entry points had been identified. The *clean team* has named the cohort of eighteen *Ghostbuster Geckoes*. They're so ravenous for dinner they're climbing out of their box and lining up for a race. Dave has the dubious honor of setting them loose. One by one he'll place a pair of geckoes at each entry point.

"Ready, set, go."

It was an enthusiastic group of spectators that cheered for each pair. Afterwards Dalene and I joined other volunteers for hot dogs, chips, beer, and pop once the last gecko disappeared. Only a rare roach escaped becoming a meal that day. There wasn't a sighting of another roach for months. The plan had worked as hoped. Dare an escapee make an appearance it was treated prophylactically by *borrowing* a gecko from the neighborhood pet store. Elbert's home was less likely to attract roaches and Jim's respiratory condition stabilized. Apparently cleaning at the Elberts became an annual event. Roaches disappeared. Eventually the gathering turned into the neighborhood's Juneteenth tradition. Wonder what happened to the geckoes?

10 Finding Home

*All you need is the plan, the road map, and the
courage to press on to your destination*
— Earl Nightengale

IN THE DAYS BEFORE GARMIN and GPS, finding homes could be
problematic and time consuming. Homecare nurses would be
assigned a new patient and make a call to set a time and get
directions to the residence. Even now with GPS locating a home
care patient's residence can be problematic.

"This is Angie Bowers the home care nurse from Care At
Home. Dr. Anders has asked us to provide a little help after your
surgery. I'd like to visit tomorrow. Can you tell me how to get to
your place?"

He proceeds with the typical long-winded story of how to get
to the house.

"Mr. Farmer I can't seem to find the house."

"Oh, that's OK sweetie, sometimes it can be a little tricky. Did
you come to the end of main street then ease to one lane toward
Milliken?" shouts Mr. Farmer into the phone as if it were the
rural party line of 1923.

"Uh huh, then turned right – north to Sunflower Road."

"Oh, there's the trouble. It's a left on Sunflower. No, you
should have been going south. Try it again. Go just a little way
and you'll see the yellow mailbox with the rooster painted on it.
Turn in the drive there."

Homes are located everywhere. Finding the home is an entirely different matter given the long litany of places where you might find them. In neighborhoods, gated communities, lifestyle centers, mobile home parks, retirement villas, farms, ranches, senior living apartments, subsidized housing, barrios, colonias, ghettos, homeless shelters, tenements, flats, walkups, condos, townhomes, hogans, motels, mansions, cabins, houseboats, and lake houses. Fascinated by how and why towns and cities were named I began to track where the homes I visited were located and looking up their story. Albany, Belzoni, Chesapeake, Duluth, El Paso, Jackson, Poughkeepsie, Raleigh, Utica, Winnemucca, Williston, Xenia, Youngstown, Zuni. Follow a few adventures of trying to find a home or agency.

Jenny was my first navigator before Siri showed up many years later. As a Research Assistant for our home health study team at the University she coordinated my trips out of state. That meant scheduling flights, purchasing tickets, booking rental cars, and making reservations for lodging. MapQuest became available in 1996 and had been in wide use by the time I started traveling in 1999. As backup she used the now almost extinct 3ft. Rand McNally paper map and a plastic ruler to calculate miles from location to location. Jenny created a detailed itinerary listing hotel and agency addresses and phones, numbers of rental car companies, driving directions (in addition to Map Quest) and local emergency numbers along the route. All carefully organized into a travel binder. 911 went into place in the United States in 1968 but not all municipalities were connected. Hard to imagine, isn't it?

Flip phones, that now rightly belong in technology museums, had only been in use for three years. While stranded for three days at Newark airport Holiday Inn by a *once in a century* snowstorm I occupied the time learning how this strange device operated while snowplows delivered food and fellow travelers played cards and swapped travel stories. Tips about flip phones were freely exchanged. Audible tutorials via the internet were still in the future. Instructions about how to use your phone were hidden underneath WARNINGS, that were frightening to read. Just for safety's sake I continued carrying extra change - that would be dimes and quarters - for pay telephones in areas where cell phone coverage was poor or non-existent, especially in rural areas.

Hallo home care nurses who are reading this. Take a few minutes to smile, remembering your adventures; where you were, where you were trying to go and the many comical stories, or not, about finding homes. I gave up saying *I have GPS, so I'll be just fine*. It doesn't deter the obligatory long-winded directions. Detailed explanations about how to get to where they live.

"....So, after you cross Ten Mile Road, you'll see a pond. That's the pond where old McPherson's barn used to be. Now they got those wind things all on the hillside. Far as your eyes can see. Still raising corn, they are. We're about two miles straight from there. What time did you say you were coming?"

"Ah, well let's see. You're at the Gulf station by Marylou's cafe, right? Turn left out of Marylou's parking lot; you'll be going west. Then go till you see Richardson's green barn with the quilt squares painted on the side. It's only five more turn-ins to where you turn left, curve around the hog shed, go past the dirt entry into the windmill. Peterson's farm is on the right, we're on the left."

Then there are those times when you find the residence and not the patient. I was to meet the patient's nurse at the Illinois farmhouse where Eleanor Sheridan was born seventy-six years ago. Margo arrived at the same time I did.

"Oh, forgot to tell you, Miss Sheridan may not be at the house."

"Doctor appointment?"

Miss Sheridan is recovering from open heart surgery nine days earlier, and Margo is visiting to assess how the incisions are healing. Under Medicare home care regulation patients are to remain homebound while they are receiving home care. That is, patients are restricted from leaving the home except for healthcare appointments. Otherwise, the agency has to discharge them.

"Whoo Hoo Woo Hoo."

Climbing down from a classic green Deere tractor, circa 1950s, Eleanor is hailing us from the middle of a plot of land adjacent to the farmhouse. She's slapping dirt from her work gloves. She and Josephine, her sister, tend a five-acre vegetable garden and fruit orchard that was once part of a farm homesteaded by their grandfather. The sisters have contracted help for planting and harvesting the soy bean crop. What a delightful character. Margot completed her assessment and obtains a *cross my heart hope to die* promise from Eleanor not to ride the tractor for two more weeks. With a twinkle in her eye as she waves good-bye.

"I was going to go to the hardware store. Guess I better keep my promise. Not too fond of the alternative."

It wasn't unusual to have trouble locating the agency itself. Many factors influence where an agency chooses to locate a business office. Regulatory requirements, availability of affordable commercial space, budgeting, accessibility to patients. Hospital-based home care agencies are often difficult to locate in a maze of hallways in the main hospital, usually in the basement. Or off-site. Freestanding for-profit agencies can be tucked in corners of shopping centers, *by JC Penney*. Some are in private homes until owners can afford to move to a commercial office space. Humboldt County Home Care's address was listed at the public health office. I finally found the agency in a large, corrugated steel building at the edge of town.

Alan Schroeder, Administrator, was noticeably missing too when I arrived at the appointed time, so the assembled staff and I continued our friendly conversation. He'd purchased ten remote monitoring units, and this was the first day of training and home placements.

"He's delayed at a hog confinement," said Sally Eggers, Nursing Director. Alan soon arrived, we shook hands and said hello. He apologized for the delay and removed his muddy Wellingtons.

"How did it go?" asks several nurses.

"Very well. Very well. A young new farmer." I must have looked quite puzzled.

"Just what is a hog confinement for us city folks?"

"Oh, I'm sorry. I'm on the state board of agriculture and part of my responsibility is to survey new and remodeled hog barns and sheds, confinements, to confirm they meet health and safety regulations."

Coincidently, one of the monitors was placed at the farm Alan visited that morning. The young farmer was the patient's grandson. Mr. Ellison's health had recently deteriorated, and a nurse was visiting twice a week; forty miles round trip. Remote monitoring was a perfect solution for this agency as there were times when nurses were making visits long distances. Both Mr. Ellison and his grandson caught on quickly and could complete a monitoring session easily.

"I'm so relieved that someone will be checking how he's doing every day. He's really had a bad time of it recently."

Unlike Eleanor Sheridan who was home, Ed Winter wasn't. He was reportedly dead in his lower east side apartment in Manhattan.

"Are you looking for Ed? He's dead up there. We haven't seen him for days. It'd be just like 'im, that old cuss. Nope, haven't seen him. He could be down at the soup kitchen."

Climbing the outside stairway and knocking on the window repeatedly didn't make him appear. He was known to come and go unpredictably. Still, I was concerned. He'd had a cardiac arrest a year ago. A call to the soup kitchen confirmed he was chatting away and telling tall tales about his glory days on Broadway.

When I called Mr. Mitchell to schedule the visit in Carmel-by-the-Sea CA, I think I've misunderstood.

"Is there a specific address Mr. Mitchell?" I ask.

"No, can't say we've ever had addresses."

That turns out to be true. There are no street addresses and properties are identified by location. Carmel-by-the-Sea has the distinction of having street names but no numbers. The home is referred to as *two houses from the corner of North and San Antonio St. on the southwest corner*. How interesting. I scheduled a visit at Miramar, two blocks from downtown on Heron Ct. After roaming up and down a two-block perimeter setting off the downtown quarter, there it is. A driftwood sign artistically decorated with seashells clearly displays where I'm supposed to be, Miramar – The Mitchells.

Some homes float. Surprisingly, although technically not land bound, they have regular street addresses that correspond to the wharf side location and are identified by the number of its anchorage slip. For example, 10700 Meridian Ave. #504. In visiting with home care nurses in Seattle I learn visits to elderly clients living in houseboats aren't that common. However, it's not unusual to visit adults recovering after surgeries or accidents or other medical conditions.

Directions to other homes are connected to visual markers.

"It's on the fourth floor. When you park in the lot just look up and we're the condo with the pink flamingos on the balcony."

"… you'll see Chili's in front of the motel. I'm the room right in the middle. We sit out most of the day in the shade to stay cool. Air conditioning hasn't been working. I'll watch for you."

"Be sure you use the wood plankway to get to the beach house."

"Please close the cattle gate securely."

"After you turn off the main road it's a steep drive up to the house. Best to use low gear."

"This time of year, the bridge to the cabin may be washed out."

"I'm in a double wide. White boulders line the driveway." As they do every mobile home space.

"Don't leave any food in the car; we have bears."

"My wife loves those cement goose lawn ornaments. You'll know the house. I think they're wearing Halloween costumes now."

MapQuest paper directions worked just fine for the time being. Large cities were a conundrum trying to read the next line in time to make the correct turn. Nuvi-Garmin was the next device that helped nurses reach a destination. It functioned on satellite Global Positioning Systems (GPS) not cell towers. Smart phones now have standard maps apps. MapQuest and Google Maps. iPhone has an internal GPS. I still appreciate good old fashioned verbal directions too. GPS revolutionized finding homes and has a set of stories of its own. To be told by today's practicing home health nurses…wherever they are and wherever they go.

11 Broadleaf Maple Flag

Feel the magic of Canada.

HOME IS EVERYWHERE wouldn't be complete without a nod to our northern neighbors. In 2008 and 2009 I travelled to western Canada. The Canadian Health Service purchased American made remote telehealth monitors and I was there to help home health nurses implement and support a customized telehealth program for British Columbia and Alberta. That assignment was one of the high points of my home healthcare life. In this tiny hermitage where I now live and write, an entire wall showcases photos of those Canadian adventures. Fanny Bay Oyster shells are on display as are photos of indigenous totems at ghostly villages and purple starfish clinging to rocks in tidepools. A black felt over-the-shoulder medicine pouch embroidered with the Butterfly Clan symbol, given to me by descendants of the Kwakiutl tribe, claims an honored space on the wall.

"It was fitting. You are Butterfly Clan too," says Winona as she puts the bag across my shoulder. "Tradition holds that Butterfly Clan women were healers (and still are) who collected and stored herbs in their felt bags. You have brought us good medicine."

A misty island fog had overtaken the dense forest where George and Mary Pippin live at the end of a five-mile access road. This home is where I'll begin my discovery of the world of home healthcare on an island. Yesterday I ferried from Tsawwassen terminal, Vancouver British Columbia to Swartz Bay terminal,

Victoria, Vancouver Island. It's crisp and cool in the little town of Brackendale near Squamish where I stayed overnight.

"Take your time," Mary calls down the hall to George who is slipper shuffling from his bedroom to the dining table. A wall size picture window showcases views of a vast lawn that hugs the riverside.

"Is it all right if I set this box on the dining table? It holds the remote monitoring unit I've brought to install." Mary's carrying a teapot dressed in its quilted chintz tea cozy to the table.

"Go right ahead, do you have enough room to unpack the monitor?" Mary asks, pausing in mid-pour. Mmmm! steaming Earl Grey.

"Is this your first time here to Vancouver Island?"

Pausing in mid-answer nothing is coming out of my mouth. Across the lawn past the red alder trees at the edge of an old growth forest dozens of bald eagles are coming and going. Too many to count. These are massive birds. George is smiling at my astonishment.

"Oh, you should see them in January. Hundreds. We've lived here forty-five years and every day there's something to see. Building nests, feeding nestlings salmon from the nearby Squamish River. Once I saw an eaglet learning to fly that lost its grip and swung upside down on a branch, wings spread wide. It didn't seem to know what to do. After a bit of flapping, it let go, took off and somehow landed upright on a lower branch. Mary has her own thoughts on the eagles."

"I have no doubt it was the eagles that helped my George recover after his stroke. We moved the table out and put his hospital bed facing the window. Little by little, as he watched, his left arm got stronger over the weeks. Strong enough to hold binoculars.

"Watching those eagles seemed to lift his spirits. Now he's able to sit in the yard to watch. Being outdoors in fresh air is healing too."

Reluctantly we take our gaze off this convocation of eagles and get busy installing the remote monitor. Home healthcare nurses are the ones who will tell you:

"It's straight forward, people get better faster at home. We're the ones who see it. We don't have to see research data to confirm it's true. People recover faster and better at home, especially when they can be outdoors. What's even more interesting is that a return to health and recovery is enhanced when birds are part of the story. Mental and physical health improves."

My first visit to Alberta took me to Ft. McMurray, located in the middle of the Athabascan oil fields that are surrounded by hundreds of kilometers of boreal forest. At that time the population was about 40,000 permanent residents and swelled to over 100,000 if oil fields workers were counted. Flying in via Alaska Air just a little after 8 p.m. I checked in to the Radisson, Ft. McMurray's only hotel. It was the first available reservation for two months.

"Just to let you know, Ma'am. It may be around eleven, maybe midnight before our restaurant will be able to seat you. We only have two servers, forty-five on the wait list and we're waiting on the last flight of the day with groceries. They'll ring your room a half hour before they expect your table to be ready." He's unhurried and pleasant. This must be a regular occurrence.

"Excuse me is there a Walmart nearby? I forgot my black pants."

"Uh Oh – better hurry. Fifteen minutes until the last semi is unloaded. Expect a line at the door."

Women's clothing is in the far outreaches of the store. Four remaining pairs of pants are pathetically hanging limp. Petite, LG, XL, and two XXL. I grabbed the XL, two sizes larger than Medium which I wear. And needle and thread for altering.

Next day I meet home care nurses at Northern Lights Regional Health Center in Ft. McMurray. We plan out our days ahead. Over lunch I get a briefing on the prehistoric and current history of the area. We call it a day early as everyone wants to get home to take their kids to ice hockey and fix dinner. Homecare's curling team is defending its title at 9pm.

I'm curious about what tar sands mining is about and decided to take a drive out to the oil fields to take a look. I see nothing but what appears to be a wasteland. Suddenly from nowhere, Trailways buses pour out of the horizon. A total of a hundred and four buses are leaving Exxon Mobile, Imperial, Suncor/Sunoco, Shell, BP, Conoco petroleum operations to single wide housing trailers close to Ft. McMurray.

I drove another five miles to where active oil sands are being mined. It makes me sick. Not the smell of oil, though it permeates the air, but the destruction of the land makes me want to cry. Like a scene from a Star Wars movie four gargantuan steel monsters, each larger than an AT-AT walker, rape the surface of the earth with a massive claw shovel and scoop lumps of sand into waiting dump trucks for transporting to crushers for processing. Once the tar sand is crushed, chemicals and hot water are added so it can be pumped to a bitumen extraction plant.

Next day RN Marylou Kitchens and I are making monitor installation home visits. She tells me the history of tar sands mining and how residents of Ft. Mc Murray who worked in the fields have been affected. Melvin Whitaker, our first telehealth installation, has chronic pulmonary disease and stomach cancer. He worked only a few years at the processing plant. But even short-term exposure can increase the risk of cancer and respiratory disease. Melvin's a good candidate for remote monitoring.

Remote telemonitoring is particularly suitable for extending healthcare to First Nation tribes who are isolated by distance and weather. First Nation Community centers are a critical link to health care, so the next day we make a visit to the Clearwater Reserve near Anzac. We arrived at the Athabascan Tribal Council Administration Community Center where Cree elders are speaking among themselves in their native dialect. Today the buzz is that nurse Jan from Northern Lights is bringing something to help Ayamis, *one who has stars for a blanket.* Ayamis, an LPN, holds a weekly blood pressure and diabetic foot care clinic. There's a well-established set of protocols for coordinating health care in the province. Jan visits every two weeks to review Ayamis' health logs and assess various members of the tribe with chronic diseases and non-emergent illnesses. Tar sands chemicals are linked to higher rates of cancer in indigenous communities. Dangerous air pollution has blanketed the entire Athabascan landscape since 1967 when extraction began. Community centers are a hub of an indigenous community.

Ayamis will use the remote monitor for the weekly clinic. Readings are transmitted to a Central Station at Northern Lights hospital in Ft. McMurray. Additionally, the monitor can be used anytime to send readings to the clinic's physician, also located in Ft. McMurray. In this setting where access to care is hampered by distance, the monitor can assist in triaging whether a Cree tribal member should be taken to Ft. McMurray or can remain at home in the reserve. During the winter months roads can become impassable.

Hot lunch is served to seniors midday and everyone remains for afternoon activities, friendship, and conversation. Lunch is over when we arrive from Ft. McMurray. Conversation stops, everyone looks up. Keasik, *sky blue*, has been chosen to go first because, at age 96, she's the oldest. Everyone rearranges their chairs to face a plate glass window that separates the clinic from the day room. Keasik is proudly smiling and enjoys the honor, waving at friends in the audience. After I demonstrate how a monitoring session is done, Ayamis takes Keasik's readings. People clap. At age 91 Mahikan, *wolf*, the oldest male elder goes next. One by one we successfully get everyone to use the monitor at least once. Some want to try it again. Conversations grow more animated.

"Keasik wonders would you like to see the shawl she is

embroidering for her great-great-great granddaughter Mia," whispers her 80 yr. old sister.

"That would be very special."

"We'd like that very much," says Jan.

A brilliant peacock color satin cape reaching from shoulders to moccasin heels is edged with silver tassels. Today Keasik is embroidering a pair of snowshoe hares on the back of the cape using silver thread. A labor of love for Mia's first performance at the Ft. McKay Pow Wow in September. Keasik tells about when she first danced at powwow.

"Like this." She raises her arms as if she were flying and her cape is flowing like wings of a soaring eagle.

As we leave, Mahikan shakes my hand, pressing into it a miniature carved loon.

"From the tribe."

12 Birdseed and Fancy Feast

We do not remember days, we remember moments.

"MOM, GRANDPA IS EATING my sand dollar from California!"

This is a story about the kindest, gentlest, happy man with Alzheimer's. Caring for a loved one with Alzheimer's is one of the most heartbreaking responsibilities someone may have. It also takes a special kind of home care nurse to help families cope. A home care nurse who became her father's primary caregiver tells a story about a seven-year journey through the ups and downs of Alzheimer's. Eating a sand dollar was only one of the memories she and her family cherishes.

It all began in California. A cool ocean breeze drifts through palm trees here at Del Mar thoroughbred horse racing track in San Diego. It's August. A bugle call announces horses entering the oval track from the paddock where jockeys have mounted up for the fifth race. Azaleas and floral Birds of Paradise frame a colonial Spanish clubhouse surrounded by manicured green lawns that fade into the Pacific blue. We're here to visit Dad's sister who lives in Escondido. He's studying the Daily Racing Form to pick this race's winner.

"Here, you pick," he says handing me the Form.

I'm surprised. It was this trip to Del Mar that I knew. He kept looking down at the Racing Form then his eyes would look up and to the right. He didn't know where he was or what he was supposed to be doing. He had been one of the best handicappers at Centennial racetrack in Littleton. When we went to the paddock to watch the jockeys saddle up for the next race he thought he was working with his dad, a teamster, who was stablemaster for twenty-five horses that pulled Happy Home Bakery wagons in Denver in the 1920s.

Alzheimer's sneaks up on families of loved ones. In the late 1990s, although the disease was recognized, little was definitively known, other than it was slow and progressive. Geriatrics was an emerging medical practice and geriatricians were beginning to understand that Alzheimer's is a type of dementia. A constellation of signs and symptoms all somehow tied to changes in the brain that consequently affected memory and ultimately ability to function.

After Del Mar I continued to travel out-of-state weekly for work. Dad remained in his home for 40 years. During the six years he had been a widower he spent his days thriving in the outdoors and the mountains where he would fish and hike. Revisiting places he'd frequented for seventy years. Each year in September he looked forward to driving two hundred and thirty miles to Meeker, Colorado for the annual Meeker Classic Sheepdog trials. Over the years he became friends with most of the handlers and judges who came from across the U.S. and Scotland and looked forward to seeing them. He loved the border collies and knew them all by name. It became a family tradition and a special weekend for all. In later years I drove him until he was too frail.

Predictably the next stages of Alzheimer's began to progress. I knew what the future looked like and early on I entertained the possibility of buying a three-bedroom home and having a live-in caregiver. My goal was to keep him safe in his own home as long as possible. Selling his home to move to a house he didn't know seemed cruel. Making decisions about changing living settings is a difficult decision family caregivers must often face.

One weekend when I was home, Ernie, a neighbor of Dad's, hailed me at the gas station.

"Saw your dad having breakfast at Crestwood the other day. Well, it was the car I saw. That old thing is getting pretty banged up."

"It's been his life since he was fifteen. I think he realizes his drives to the mountains are over."

Everyone around town recognized Blue Boat, a 1975 two-door navy blue Ford LTD. First new car he'd ever purchased. For years he and Mom drove to Las Vegas every year. He drove alone to Vegas the summer after she was gone. He and Blue Boat survived. It must have been difficult. Eventually the passenger door didn't latch shut and finally wouldn't open so he taped it shut with a roll of silver duct tape. Once a week he chauffeured his two brothers, ages 72 and 74, to lunch at their favorite place, the Apple Tree. Under the circumstances they crawled into the back seat through the driver's door. What a comical scene. Like an old Three Stooges movie. Eventually those outings weren't possible. He couldn't remember the way home. Dad continued to drive a half mile to the grocery store, or Crestwood, a family restaurant, or dinner at Romano's Italian. I don't know how many times he took out the planters getting into a parking spot at the shopping center. As more planters went missing and dents in Blue Boat increased, he suggested that maybe he should give his car to my daughter. I think he was relieved.

Helping families cope with a loved one who is no longer capable of driving safely is a time when it's OK to let the nurse be the *bad guy*. There's no perfect way to manage this sad situation. Taking car keys or selling the car abruptly is traumatic for everyone, even if it's necessary. In a way, it's a process, a grieving process. A visible reality that the person is losing the last fragment of their independence. It's ideal to start a conversation before it's a crisis. It's important that family and caregivers are united in the decision that their loved one stops driving. It could seem that talking about the car might be just the wrong thing to do. But sometimes it helps. Dad spent hours talking about his first car.

Engines he repaired on his mother's dining table, road trips with his brother, and honeymoon with Mom. Our trip to California when I was five. No matter how you say it, it's never easy. Maybe just be honest.

"It must feel like this is the worst that could ever happen. I wish I could make it different. Truly I do. But you can't drive anymore."

Maybe your loved one can tell you stories about their cars. Open the conversation. *Tell me about your first car? What model was it?* the conversation takes off from there.

Sometimes the home care nurse is the one who needs to makes the first move. I've been successful with this strategy.

"Tell you what, give me your car keys. I'll have a surprise for you."

I ask a family member, friend, or caregiver to purchase a shadow box frame and place a photo of a loved one standing by their car, or truck; vintage or recent. Glue the ignition key and gas cap inside the frame and hang it in a visible place. Remove it if it causes the person to become angry or confused. There are many creative ways to ease the loss of independence.

Prior to the time Dad stopped driving I received a call from King's Supermarket.

"Hello, is this Mr. Smith's daughter? I found your name on the checks. I'm Jerry, manager up at King's. I thought you might want to know your dad is writing a check every day for a 2lb can of coffee, ten pounds of birdseed and ten cans of Fancy Feast."

"Oh dear, I'll look into it," I assured him.

We were blessed that Dad was safe at home for four years after Del Mar. Initially he loved fixing his own meals and treating our family to a picnic every July 4th at his place to watch nearby fireworks. He was happy and content with his days. Up early making coffee. His vision was poor so most of the coffee ended up on the floor. Sitting in front of a large kitchen window as the sun came up, he said morning prayers while watching *my little bird friends* and writing poems before fixing breakfast or going to Crestwood. Moses, a twenty-pound white purebred Persian cat lazed across a window bench Dad built for him.

We just lived day by day, week by week trying to keep Dad home as long as possible. Each week before I left on Monday for work, I filled small manilla envelopes with pills for each day of the week. The day of the week was written on each envelope with a black marker. I drew happy sun faces on morning pills' envelopes and evenings had a crescent moon with a smile. My daughters took turns coming every evening to make sure he had something to eat for dinner. They would sit with him at the table and visit for a little while, check that morning envelopes were empty and watch as he took his evening pills. After a hug they left him smiling and waving goodbye as they backed down the driveway. A cousin regularly took him fishing at Deckers on the South Platte River where Dad learned to fish as a ten-year-old. On weekends we drove to all his favorite places in the mountains.

"What's that place?" he'd ask. "I've seen it before."

We never tired of the stories he told repeatedly. The day finally came. It was inevitable. We would have to sell the house to finance the years ahead. With Alzheimer's, the number of years a person might live is unpredictable and long-term care would be needed. It was best to sell in the Spring, so we started downsizing in January. He was the center of the process as we went through eighty years of his life. My children and I spent weekends at the house. I was determined not to do what so many families often do. Move the person and then go through everything and dispose of mementoes at a garage sale. Another sad mistake families make is arguing or trying to convince a loved one with Alzheimer's about facts.

"No, we didn't go there. We lived in north Denver, not Englewood."

"That's not true."

"You don't go to work anymore."

"We've heard that story before."

And we didn't use the words *when did that happen?*

"When did that happen?" The details aren't important.

Tell me about that unlocks a world of cherished memories.

We learned so much about his life by asking,

"Tell us about that time…. Dad."

People with Alzheimer's are frightened they can't remember dates, but they love to tell a story about something that happened. Over the weeks each of the four grandchildren sat with Dad and keepsakes were spoken for and antique furniture was taken to a storage unit. Before the For Sale sign went up, we spent weekends clearing out. David sat with Dad in the backyard dragging contents from a shed out onto the lawn. Among stacks of newspapers there were carpenter's tools from the 1920s, and fishing gear. Framed photos of winners from various horse races at Centennial. Programs from the Sheep Dog Trials. Callie began trimming up the yard, repairing the platform bird feeder, and loading rocks Dad had brought home from the mountains – rocks that now form a grotto on my patio. David and Callie will never forget the stories he told that spring day. Stories that are now told (and retold) at family gatherings.

"Oh my God, come look at this. You'll never believe it."

Monika is in a bedroom and has just opened the closet. Dozens of Meals on Wheels lunches and paper plates with leftover dinner come tumbling out. As she tries to catch them, she realizes that food is still in them. All those evenings she was backing down the driveway and he was waving and smiling he was headed to the bedroom.

Almost simultaneously my son Callie yells from the backyard, "Wait till you see this!"

April snow has started to melt and what seemed to be mounds of snow are mounds of birdseed. Dad couldn't remember if he had fed the birds so he would take another can of seed to spread on the birdfeeder platform. No wonder there were so many pigeons in the neighborhood. Callie filled three fifty-gallon trash barrels with the piled seed. That explained the daily check to the store. And the twenty-pound Persian cat? Dad couldn't remember if he had fed Moses. Of course, Moses licked the bowl clean every time Fancy Feast was put into it.

Sadly, not all those with Alzheimer's are as happy as Dad was. Many can be mean and aggressive, and the memories aren't pleasant. But remember the happy days, even if few. At a recent family gathering a grandson recalled.

"Remember that time Grandpa tried to eat a sand dollar I collected in Malibu? He thought it was a sugar cookie."

This is a true story. I'm the daughter. The University of Colorado Health Sciences Center for Healthcare Policy was under contract with the Department of Health and Human Services to draft and create training materials that would support the emerging payment system. I represented the researchers as homecare Subject Matter Expert for the creation of a set of eighteen video scripts as tools for training on the OASIS assessment. I traveled to Newport News VA intermittently for three years to film the videos. The production team won national Communicator and Telly awards and I was awarded separate ones for script writing based on this story.

13 Tasting Cultures

Every Culture Has A Story

"I'LL MAKE US A CUPPA," says Nurse Franklin in the hit British TV series *Call the Midwife*. A baby is born, a frantic father is calmed, an immigrant grandmother is reassured, a Mom pregnant for the sixth time cries. Something so simple, yet profound as a cup of tea. Food brings people together on many levels. Food is the cornerstone of those human interactions. *You have to taste a culture to understand it.* says Deborah Cater, a travel writer. As we in home care travel home to home, neighborhood to neighborhood, and city to city, stories of those we meet come alive. Often, those stories are revealed while sharing food. The following snippets offer a taste of a few cultures.

Honoring a Filipino Grandmother

Bang! An iron gate slams shut behind me. A hanging basket of drooping English ivy is at eye level and instinctively I duck. A pair of impish brown eyes peer between flaming red window curtains as a subterranean level door opens. A boy about twelve becomes visible. Dressed in pressed khakis, short sleeved white shirt, and royal blue bow tie he appears misplaced from some private British boy's school.

"I'm Ernesto. I got to stay home from school today so I can translate," he smiles.

A plump gnome-like white haired woman steps forward from behind the door.

"Kaumsta kayo," I sputter.

My attempt to say hello in Tagalog (Filipino) is pitiful. Ernesto is trying to stifle a laugh, but it bubbles up in his throat and chortles out his nose. She eyes me warily and wipes her hands on a crisp white apron that's over a bright flowered, probably Sunday, dress. She accosts me with a round tin of paper-thin rolled sugar cookies. She's made a special trip to the market and used a little money from her Social Security check.

"My lola (grandmother) asks will you have some tea and cookies."

"Oh, no thanks. I'm fine."

I have no idea that I've just made a terrible cultural mistake. Refusing an offer tea or cookies is offensive and certainly not a good start for establishing trust.

"Let's see how your grandfather is doing."

Ernesto's lolo (grandfather), Mr. Armando Reyes, is trying to sit up in bed. As Ernesto helps me ease him to sitting on the edge of the bed, I'm asking questions as I always do.

"How are you feeling? Have you walked a little today?" I mime the words as I mimic walking my first and second fingers across the palm of my other hand. "Let's see, are your feet more swollen?"

As Mr. Reyes responds and Ernesto translates, Grandmother comes up behind Ernesto and starts whacking him on the back with a folded newspaper.

"You tell nurse what I say! Not what he says!"

So, we proceed. I ask a question. Ernesto translates. First to lola then to lolo; Ernesto looks to lolo then lola and then translates to me. Ernesto has a way of winking at me and then nodding his head toward the one who's telling the real truth. My head swivels back and forth like an owl watching a mouse run back and forth on the forest floor. I feel like one of those bobblehead dolls. I'm dizzy by the time I'm finished. He and I transfer lolo to the recliner and we leave him watching the Filipino soccer team play Jordan on the TV. Thankfully I remember the word thank you.

"Salamat."

Midway through the visit I realized how disrespectful I was earlier.

"Shall we have tea and cookies now?" I ask.

Grandmother has already set out the tin and the teapot is steaming. Precious family stories find their way into a conversation. Tagalog and English interlace and both of us look to Ernesto to make sure I understand what she is trying to share with me. She asks if I have grandchildren. That prompts her to talk about how she worries over her children and grandchildren and the love of her life in the recliner. Teacups are refilled. To make sure I eat as many cookies as possible she scootches the tin across the table for me to take. She stands up and grabs my hand with her two hands and walks me to the door and drops a baggie of cookies in my purse. We part on a goodbye; *Paalam*. Ernesto follows me up the outside steps past the ivy.

"Will you come tomorrow again so I can get out of school?"

Acceptance Over Borscht

Dimitri, a gadget person, and engineer with degrees in technology and business was swept away at a recent American Telemedicine convention by the possibilities of remote telemonitoring. He couldn't resist and ordered twenty monitors for their home health agency that he and his wife Inga own. They emigrated from Ukraine and care for upper income patients in the Russian Jewish community in the Hollywood CA area. Inga, a highly skilled master's prepared RN wants to increase referrals from Russian physicians who already trust her. Only Dmitri is enthused about his purchase. The nursing staff, however, are skeptical. Anya,

Irina, Katya, and Luda are beautiful young nurses adored by their patients. Everyone else growled about it and predicted it wouldn't work.

"Our patients will never accept such a thing. No, no, no."

Today we're making home visits. Irina is with me to learn how to install a monitor and explain how it works. Our first patient is Alina Semenov whose three daughters are shouting and waving their arms around for emphasis. Arguing seems to be a necessary component of decision making. Alina's wish to have a monitor wins out. I suspect her wishes would win most discussions. She wants to be the first babushka (old woman/grandmother) in her friendship circle to have a monitor. She wants to please Dimitri and Inga too. Movie posters signed by the famous Russian actress Mila hang on the living room walls. There she is snuggling right up to Bruce Willis.

"Don't ask her about her granddaughter. We'll be here all day," whispers Irina. Dimitri joins Irina and I after the visit and insists we stop at Traktir, a famous Russian restaurant.

"Try borscht," he suggests. "It comes with every meal."
The conversation turns to the ups and downs of starting a home care agency. What is set in front of me is a clear ruby red broth with beef, shredded red cabbage, and sliced beets, a steaming hot soup with a nostalgic aroma that reminds me of the pot roast with carrots my dad cooked for Sunday dinner.

It continues to be an extraordinary three days in every way. I'm impressed watching these expert nurses interacting with their patients. Patient teaching is a major part of home health nursing. Here, the approach is surprisingly opposite from an American approach. On a home visit with Luda, she puts one hand on her hip, takes a defiant stand and starts putting her stethoscope in her bag with the other hand. We just got here. She points her finger at the patient.

"What!!! Do you want to die.!!! You don't take your medicine, so what am I supposed to do, huh? I might as well go home."

Surprise! The entire staff has gathered this last day for a potluck of traditional Russian and Ukrainian foods is spread out in the conference room. Over borscht we talk about what healthcare and home care is like in Russia and Ukraine; the incidence of diabetes and heart disease. Challenges they face here in serving an affluent community and differences in home health care around the world. There's a hidden tension when talking about families. Several nurses have families in Crimea and the Donbas region in Ukraine and they're worried about possible hostilities. Inga slipped two fresh loaves of Nareznoy bread into my carry-on bag, so you'll remember us.

I have remembered them and even more so when Russia invaded Ukraine in February 2022 causing thousands of civilian injuries and deaths and displacing millions of refugees. I hope and pray that the families of Dmitri, Inga and all their Ukrainian staff are alive and safe.

Cucumber Mourning

It's not uncommon for home care nurses to have a caseload of patients in a particular area of town. My coverage area is a large community of Vietnamese and Cambodian refugees. Vietnamese elders sit against a living room wall cross-legged; each on a carpet square. Incense burns. A bedroom door opens and closes quietly. Footsteps pad across the hall to the bathroom to refill a large basin of warm water. Trang Lanh Sang is dying. This is expected. Children and grandchildren will come and go. Elders will arrive early in the day and stay till evening. Someone will stay through the night. Cousins and those who are special to Trang have been invited to come to say goodbye. Trang is growing weaker every day. He has had a long life with many remembrances of the life before coming to America. As he weakens everyone tells the stories. His American sponsor, responsible for his secret escape from Cambodia, comes from California.

Yun, a granddaughter, takes me aside and explains that in their culture death isn't the end, but a final stage of this life to be transformed into the next. As early as 1624 French Catholic missionaries converted the Vietnamese people, and a row of flickering red holy candles burn continuously as evidence to that conversion and steadfast faith. Standing at the bar between kitchen and dining room I watch her peel and slice a giant cucumber into so many thin strips it overflows a basket. She's come home for a lunch break after class at the University. Yun is finishing a masters in sociology. Her role here is not only as a translator for me, but also to see that food is always available for those who will visit. She looks up with kind eyes. You can see the love for her people and her family.

Watching her slice one cucumber into so many strips it overflows a basket reminds me of the time Jesus fed the five thousand. I ask her how best to show respect to the visitors, when the time comes, not to participate but to honor. We tiptoe into the bedroom where Vu, her grandmother, has just bathed Trang as he lay on his mattress on the floor. They've had their private time together and now she will sit quietly next to him listening and remembering her part in the stories. One by one the elders will come and go, and Yun's basket will be filled and emptied time and time again in the coming days.

Tortilla Truce

It's 1989 North Denver. Historically a tough neighborhood of coexisting fourth generation Italian and Mexican families. Territorial clashes between rival gangs make home visits in these neighborhoods a bit dangerous. Tensions have increased with new gangs moving from Los Angeles. I place my *There are no drugs in this car* signs in front and back windows, lock my purse in the trunk although some trunks have been punched open.

"Hello, hello Mr. Jaramillo, it's your home care nurse," I call through a broken window screen on the front porch.

"Come in, come in chica (*young girl*) it's open. It's OK."

He's moving slowly down the back hallway from his locked bedroom carrying wound care supplies.

"Several visitors come and go. At night. Some stay over. I don't like these goings on. I worry about my boys."

Concerned I ask, "Are you afraid?"

"Not really – but I hear arguments. I know they have knives, maybe a gun."

On the days I visit, his daughter Gabriela leaves fresh tamales and handmade tortillas. After changing Mr. Jaramillo's leg ulcer dressing, I walk to the corner where a police storefront covered in gang graffiti has been set up in an abandoned butcher shop. It's been purposefully designated as a safe haven. This is part of a new war on crime strategy to diffuse potential confrontations. Word's gotten around that I spend time there on the days I visit Mr. Jaramillo. A truce has been established on days a home care nurse is in the neighborhood. A dialogue has also been established between police and gang leaders. Over tamales and tortillas, I'm asked some sobering questions. About birth control, a grandmother who has cancer, a dad who's had a heart attack, a pregnant girlfriend and whether a friend who's been knifed is likely to survive. Mostly I just listen.

No matter whether I've made one visit or weeks of visits to a home it's the sharing of food that seems to tie it all together, especially in the most difficult of settings.

Freedom Foods

Texas has the largest population of Nigerian-born residents and much of my home care work took place in Texas. Unrest in the African country of Biafra (Nigeria) in the 1950s led to widespread famine and the Nigerian Civil War (1967-1970.) Nigerians became refugees and immigrants. When I was putting pennies in a milk carton for children in Biafra at St. Mary's Catholic grade school in 1958 how could I have imagined I would be a guest at traditional Nigerian meals in the future.

Over the next thirty years since my pennies made it to the milk carton educated Nigerian professional men, pharmacists and physical therapists and their wives, trained midwives, came to America. A characteristic immigrant story of becoming citizens, learning the conventions and language, starting, and running a business in a foreign country and working two or three jobs.

Across tables covered in brilliant Ogbu textiles those who fled describe the terrors of civil war and determination of those who became immigrants. In many homes photos of women in Abeokuta Ladies Union traditional African dress commemorate the story of the Lioness of Lisabi, a Nigerian teacher, political campaigner, and women's rights activist of the 40's and 50's. This women's society continues, and regular meetings address women's issues. When emigrating to the U.S. cultures bring important traditions and celebrations that keep the culture strong.

I've seen photos in homes of current members and was amazed to arrive at the agency on the last day and find that the staff are all wearing traditional dress to the lunch meal. Most noticeable is a large headscarf worn as an elaborate headdress called a *gele*. At times, as the conversation turns serious, a nurse will reach across the table and take my hand. We don't know what to say so I pass Jollof rice, Moin Moin – bean pudding and iyan - pounded yam, and ogbono soup. Mango seed soup is making the rounds. I take another helping of fried sweet potato. My favorite is grilled chicken kabobs called suyi. Mostly what I've learned is that the Nigerian people are a happy people who smile broadly and laugh heartily even with a history of civil war, trying to adapt to a sometimes-inhospitable new home in a foreign country.

Posole and Potica

It's the week between Christmas and New Year's and snowflakes are drifting through a tall spruce hung with colored lights on the front lawn. Luminarias line both sides of the block marking a twenty-year tradition. Bob Vallejo, manager at Family Dollar, donates two hundred brown lunch sacks and votive candles. A local hardware store offers discounts on bags of sand to fill the bottom of each brown luminaria to anchor its lit candle. Scents of cinnamon and raisins tightly rolled into potica drift from Italian kitchens. Mexican kitchens are filled with aroma of menudo and posole simmering on the stove for New Year's Eve. It's a tradition to bring good health in the new year. I schedule more time into my home visits the week between Christmas and New Year's. Taking time to exchange holiday greetings.

"Aren't I pretty in my Christmas dress?" A six-year-old dances in front of me as I take her grandmother's blood pressure.

"No more cookies before dinner," Says a mom giving a tender slap on a hand. It's getting too dark outside so two brothers come inside to play basketball in the living room. A good thing we moved to the kitchen table where they're grandfather is sitting and I'm listening to his lung sounds for congestion.

"I got a laser sword just like Luke Skywalker." Using both hands Carlos, age seven, slices the air with a glowing *pretend* saber, knocking over the chair that's holding my nursing bag. I first met the family when Maria, the mom, had a complicated Caesarean Section a year ago. It was a challenging year. Baby Christopher was born with brain anomalies. He is dearly loved by all and is squealing in laughter at the boys playing basketball.

"Oh, here you go. Just a little something for all you've done for us," says their mom as she sends me out the door with a large Christmas bag.

Kicking off my snow boots I'm tired when I get home. It's been a long, but wonderful day of holiday spirit. Hmmm? What shall

I have to eat? Gingerbread men, pizzelles, potica, Pfeffernusse cookies, or iced sugar cookies? I'll save the menudo and posole for New Year's Eve.

14 Brotherly Love

Love each other as I have loved you…….
—John 15:12

ALVIN HAD BEEN DOREEN'S protector and superhero since she was four and he was seven. That's when the court took them away from their abusive mother and the world turned upside down. It had been that way ever since. *Together against the world* they'd say to each other. Locking pinkies, right hand palms against their hearts while pledging never ending allegiance. She called him Chip. He hated the name Alvin; the name of the father he never knew. He called her Dody. Foster home to foster home. Clarks tried hard to make them feel at home but, it was almost six months before Dody stopped biting people who stood too close. It took longer to coax her from behind Chip's back when someone spoke to her. Things went along smoothly until it came time for Chip to go to school. All hell broke loose. Finally, just to stop her crying, screaming, and kicking she was put on the bus with Chip. Both smelling of peanut butter and jelly or bologna. With a red Big Chief tablet of her own and two yellow #2 pencils she sat in the back of the classroom. More than one bloody nose from Chip's left hook and bullies got the message *Don't mess with me and my sister.*

They weren't particularly bad children; just mischievous. Harmless pranksters. Greasing the cat with Vaseline; letting the llamas escape the yard, and the guinea pigs loose in the house and putting live goldfish in the toilet. They painted the driveway purple using paint from cans found at the nearby dump. And, poured vinegar in a gallon of milk. Roaming in the junkyard was their favorite pastime. Abandoned tires that could be retreaded were rolled to the local tire repair shop bringing in a couple a' dollars for a movie. Oh! how they could laugh and run away. One summer they removed garden gnomes from neighbors' yards to a park down the block staging them as if they were playing golf. Then there was an abandoned toilet at the stop sign that sprouted stolen plastic geraniums. A much-loved black and white Border Collie named Skip appeared from somewhere and joined the two-person family. Chip started rolling Cherokee tobacco when he was thirteen. He worked at the local Ace Hardware after school where Dody sat at the back of the store doing homework and counting nails. He saved enough to buy his first car, a '53 Chevy 2-door coupe he painted robin's egg blue. Brother and sister grew up and school years came and went, more or less like other kids.

Chip was drafted and deployed to Vietnam. Both worried. She worried he wouldn't come home, and he worried she would get arrested for participating in antiwar protests. Skip laid by Chip's bedroom door and whined. Dody bought a reel-to-reel mini Penncrest tape recorder with money she earned babysitting. Each week she sent a tape to an APO address, never sure it would make it to Tan Son Nhut airbase in Ho Chi Minh City, much less to some tent in a napalmed village. She laughed and told jokes on the recording, reported the current top-ten songs, and had Skip bark into the tape deck's microphone. It was all about pretending things weren't as bad as they really were. Both let weed fog their days. Dody turned eighteen a month before Chip returned home in one piece after a second tour. They rented an apartment together using his disability income and Dody's wages as a waitress at the White Spot – home of the Big Boy Burger. By coincidence Chip met his high school shop teacher at the hardware store not long after his return.

"I hear you've been doing odd jobs for folks since you got back. Maybe you could start a handy man business. Here's $500 to get started, man. We're glad you made it home. It's a cryin' shame how people are treatin' you guys."

Word got around and it wasn't long before he'd bought a 1962 Chevy pickup and a set of basic carpentry tools. *"He's a good worker,"* they said. Dody worked mostly weekday shifts so on weekends brother and sister went fishing at Echo Lake with a six pack of Coors, ham sandwiches, and chips. Laughing and joking, reminiscing with stories of growing up. In addition to fishing they became Deadheads following Grateful Dead concert tours to Las Vegas and San Francisco.

It was December the year Chip turned forty-seven and she was forty-four that Dody noticed she was having trouble carrying orders from the restaurant kitchen to guests' tables. Since she rode the bus to work during the winter, she assumed her hands had just gotten too cold. She was enjoying her new job at Village Inn Pancake House and was now a manager. Symptoms grew worse and it took several weeks to confirm the diagnosis as Multiple Sclerosis (MS.) She was able to work another eighteen months.

A progressive autoimmune disease, MS attacks the protective sheath that covers nerve fibers. And, strangely it had recently been discovered that Denver was in a geographic area of high incidence; a Multiple Sclerosis Belt. By the time I became Dody's home care case manager several years later she had lost the ability to walk independently and spent her days in a recliner chair. A personal care aide visited early each morning transferring her from hospital bed to recliner, fixing breakfast and assisting her with personal care. Chip returned at midday to fix lunch, reposition her and refill her water jug.

Chip often stopped at historic Rock Rest Lodge in Golden on his way home to cook dinner. A group of 'Nam vets met there nightly. When he got home brother and sister watched nightly news, Wheel of Fortune and Archie and Edith Bunker re-runs after dinner. They played cards and Yahtzee and sometimes got to laughing about when they were kids.

"Remember the time we bought bus tickets to Casper Wyoming? We told the bus driver our parents were sending us to our aunt and uncle for the weekend. We told everyone at school our uncle was really rich and had the biggest ranch in Wyoming with hundreds of cows and sheep."

They closed evenings with a couple of beers followed by Chip helping Dody get ready for bed, emptying her urinary catheter bag, brushing her hair, helping her brush her teeth and wash her face. Then tucking her in for the night.

"Night, Dody."

"Night, Chip."

Locking pinkies, hands-on-hearts, pledging together for ever. There were times when Chip had one too many beers and laid awake cursing God for how their lives had turned out. It just wasn't fair. Maybe it was the invisible chip on his shoulder. It was easy to blame everything on PTSD. Maybe it was the missing front teeth or the crooked nose from too many fights. Maybe it was the cowboy boot limp from stray shrapnel all those years ago. He was a character, as my grandmother would say, rough around the edges. *Gutter language* was his dialect.

I was finishing a late afternoon visit when my pager beeped 911 and I stopped to make a phone call. The after-hours message service operator relayed the message.

Alvin Patterson's been in a crash and a nurse in the emergency room at Denver General wants you to call.

I hung up and dialed the Emergency Room known as the *knife and gun club*.

"Thanks for calling," ER nurse Deb begins. "Mr. Patterson rolled his pickup and x-rays show a fracture in one of the neck bones. Doctors are anticipating placing his skull in a halo neck brace to immobilize the spine while the neck heals. He's quite unruly and threatening to leave."

"Let me talk to him." I'm upset and angry but mostly worried.

"Look Chip, this isn't funny. It's quite serious. You could be paralyzed from the neck down. You're lucky to be alive. So, you want to have two recliners in the living room? Just cooperate! We'll get through this."

Dody's personal care worker came to the house that evening and put her to bed and another came in the morning to get her up for the day. We needed to set up a coverage schedule as Chip wouldn't be able to care for Dody as usual. No lifting.

Next morning, before the 7 a.m. shift starts, Chip removed his IV and discharged himself, halo in place. Chip sends out an SOS to a veteran buddy who picked him up and dropped him home while I'm there. Dody starts yelling and cussing as he walks through the door.

"What the hell have you done to yourself?" Chip, who looks like an alien from outer space is rather shocking in a stainless-steel contraption encircling his head and anchored to his skull with four six-inch screws. Three of eight bones in the neck have been displaced and one slight sneeze or cough could potentially cause the bones to impinge on the spinal cord paralyzing him from the neck down. I'm not sure he can tolerate ten to twelve weeks until the bones heal.

"Hold still!" I'm trying to clean his scalp around the screws with peroxide and apply antibiotic ointment.

Under his breath I hear Chip grumble. "I'll be God damn if I'm gonna wear this fuckin thing."

After four weeks Chip was approved to resume lifting Dody in and out of bed and the recliner and get her ready for bed each evening as he always did. A Village Inn breakfast aroma fills the kitchen as I come to visit using the back door. Mr. Coffee is brewing, bacon strips are sizzling in a cast iron skillet, over easy eggs are sliding around another skillet. Fresh squeezed orange juice prompts me to hum. A day *without orange juice is like a day without sunshine.* Chip is out front collecting the morning newspaper. A 1950s vintage Formica kitchen table is set. Four bloody screws are arranged on a folded napkin where the knife and fork should be. A handwritten note rests on the empty plate;

"Take these goddamn things when you go. I got no use for them."

I suspect parts of the halo that are twisted and crumpled and discarded in the trash are the work of a monkey wrench from a toolbox.

15 Animal Encounters

"Pets bring vital energy to our homes and lives.
— Laura Staley

I'M CERTAIN LILLIAN WALD and Mary Brewster, graduates of New York Hospital School of Nursing, encountered animals in 1895 as they made home visits to families in New York City's poorest immigrant neighborhoods. Their purpose was clear. *We must treat social and economic problems, not simply take care of sick people.* You got that right, Lillian. I'm not in my own neighborhood but in Houston. Social and economic ills are more than evident everywhere where I go. Struggles are a little more camouflaged in Houston's suburban neighborhoods like this one.

It's Friday. Last day of an accreditation survey. Even in the best circumstances it's a tense and tiring day made longer by flying home when I'm done. I brace myself not only for the exit interview but also the drive to the airport. Usually, my bad traffic temper settles a little by the time I blend into a swarm of grumpy business travelers. Like a weeping willow in a windstorm, I'll bend and sway as those with Friday night syndrome elbow their way to the front of the security line because of their status. I admit, my 100,000 miles a year and TSA pre-board keeps me from slumping to tears most Fridays. As it turned out, I wouldn't get home until Saturday. Not because I missed my flight, but because of Bruno.

For heaven's sake Lillian and Mary only had to contend with

starving stray dogs, feral cats, an occasional side yard of chickens and a goat or two. If you want to have a good laugh eavesdrop sometime on a table of home care nurses reminiscing by telling their stories of animal encounters.

What home healthcare nurses encounter:
- Whiskers the curious cat – aren't they all – who jumps into an open nursing bag.
- Lap dogs that think they're security dogs and bite your ankle to prove it.
- Cats who smell like walking Fancy Feast commercials.
- German shepherds who believe they're lap dogs.
- Dogs and cats that follow you to the car – and get in.
- Exotic pet snakes that have gone missing – inside.
- St. Bernard dogs that drool on your hands after you wash them.
- A dying pigeon recovered from an outside windowsill now residing inside.
- Dogs with a bad case of halitosis who breathe in your face.
- Pets that sniff opened bandages as you change a wound dressing.
- Lhasa apsos who try to get between your stethoscope and their best friend.
- Cats that tip over open pill planners and bat pills around the floor.

We've been:
- Chased by *friendly* dogs.
- Scratched, snarled, growled, and hissed at.
- Unable to leave the house because of a rattlesnake blocking the door.
- Interrupted by a seriously social cockatoo that lands on our head.

What we've heard:
- My son left their Bearded Dragon with me for the weekend.
- Oh, isn't that cute!
- He's just friendly, he won't hurt you.
- Oh, I forgot to put Spike on his leash.
- Now, go on Puff. You don't belong up there on that nurse's shoulder.
- I hope you don't mind …..
- Can you wait a minute? I can't seem to find the kids' pet rat snake.
- Well, she's a little bit timid. (NOT!)
- We haven't been able to get him to the groomer.
- I'm sorry about the poop on the kitchen floor.

What do we do?
- We bring pet food until people get their social security check. (forbidden by agency policy)
- We toss play toys as far as possible to get rid of a pesky pet.
- We fill pet dishes and clean litter boxes before we leave. (a regulation no-no)
- We take pets to no-kill shelters when elderly owners go to nursing homes or die.

I almost envy nurses with pet allergies. They're not assigned to homes with pets. The rest of us cringe when assignment information says *Please call first so Mr. Perry can lock the dog up*. Just as frightening sometimes is when you don't know there's a pet. Bruno's right up there on the list of tales I tell.

I'm sitting at the dining room table with iced tea. Lynwood Home Care is a start-up agency, and this is their first accreditation visit. Many new agencies are based in private homes until they can afford an office. Mona, the agency owner, has set up the dining room for the visit. I've been working here at the table except for the day we were out making home visits. During the week Lexi, the owner's precocious nine-year old daughter sat quietly beside me. She'd perk up when I stretched to take a break and used the time to ask a lot of questions. It wasn't annoying at all. I wish I could have spent a little more time with her. She felt it only fair to catch me up on family secrets and neighborhood gossip in exchange for showing her how a stethoscope works. We've started the exit conference. I always review how the week has gone.

"Mona, you were so well prepared. I know it seems like a long time in coming. Your patients are well cared for." She looks relieved and proud. It hasn't been an easy week for her either.

As site visits go it has been a good three days. We drove all over Houston making home visits yesterday. As usual it was a day of snarled traffic. Home visits are my favorite part of the survey. It's always a challenge to get the survey completed in three days. In addition to home visits all the policies and procedures must be reviewed. Patient records. Administrative and legal records. Accounts Payable, Billing Processes and Payroll. It's important to interview staff. I tend to carry on friendly conversations with individual employees: RNs, nurse aides, therapists, medical records staff, billing staff. It's the best way to understand how the agency processes really work.

I admire Mona, Lynwood's owner, and administrator. She's a single woman of color and mother of three who took out a sizeable loan to start the agency. It takes incredible courage, patience, and perseverance.

There's a prevailing myth that goes: *Why don't you start a home care? You can make good money.* Uh, wrong. It's the most highly regulated business in the country and there's serious fraud and abuse. The industry, as a whole, gets a bad rap. Bad apples make it even more difficult for truly legitimate and hard-working home care businesses. Staffing, orientation, training, and turnover constantly plague leadership and threaten budgets. Startup costs can sink the ship, within a year of sailing. Most, like Mona, face the risks for honorable and ethical reasons. *To bring healthcare to neighborhoods, especially the underserved.* Lillian and Mary would be proud.

Helen, director of patient care, calls to say she's stuck in traffic and isn't going to make it, so we start the Exit meeting without her. She's worked incredibly hard too. We're already running late.

An urgent call interrupts Mona. There's plenty I can do. I'll continue entering a database that records findings from the visit for the Board of Review that will determine accreditation status. Lexi comes to chat but heads outdoors. I must have looked boring. She's back in a flash screaming.

"Miss Talkington, Miss Talkington, the most terrible thing has happened. You gotta come outside and see!!"

I follow to where a yellow and white tabby kitten is desperately mewing. It can't be older than four weeks and it's dangling by its back leg between wooden slats of a 6 ft privacy fence. Its leg is pitifully twisted and bleeding.

"Hurry, Lexi, get a towel."

Its tiny heartbeat is pounding and body shaking with fright. As I wrap it there's a rumble. I feel it purring.

"Oh no! Will its leg come off?" she screams in a panic.

"No, not if I can hold it up so there's no pressure until we get the slats loose. Run and see if your mom's off the phone."

As soon as Lexi leaves, Bruno turns killer dog. Now, I'm his prey. He's furious. Crash... Slam.... Crash.... with his 160 lb. body against the fence. He's determined to leap over. Through the fence I can see his snarling teeth dripping slobber. He also eyes the kitten's leg with renewed intent.

Lexi's brothers Jeremy and Jackson have been recruited by their sister to help. They both go to the backyard, one with a stick, the other with a choke chain. What a scuffle as they chase a now terribly angry dog round and round the backyard. My arms become numb from holding the kitten above my head. Soon the crashing is against the inside of the garage and subsides as Bruno is wrestled to the basement. Both boys appear on the front lawn looking like they've barely survived a wilderness challenge course.

"I think the kitten belongs to Miss May across the street," says Lexi. "Her Matilda cat had kittens. It must have gotten out when the garage door was open. Poor little thing. How did it get over here? Bruno's a very bad dog. The neighbors keep calling the police. He bit one of Jeremy's friends. My aunt won't come over if he's in the house. Mom says he's got to go."

Mona is horrified when she comes out. We try to lessen pressure on the leg using a hammer to loosen the slats. Nope, can't pull the leg out. Mona dials Animal Control and is put on hold. She leaves a message. It's getting close to end of day, way past when I need to leave for the airport. I start hopping up and down to change position. There's no feeling in my feet and legs. When the dispatcher calls back, Mona has a little bit of trouble explaining. I hear the dispatcher wearily say, "Just what is the problem, Ma'am?" No one shows up in twenty minutes. Mona calls back.

"I'm sorry, there's only one person on call tonight. She's had to take care of a dog bite over in First Colony. Sounds like rabies – has to be seen to first. She'll get there when she can."

At dusk, the officer pulls up. When she comes to the fence she says, "Oh my God, this doesn't look good."

Together we try to ease the kitten up gently to free it. Still no luck. Stuck tight. It seems possible that leg might actually come apart. She grabs a crowbar from her truck. It takes a lot of muscle and force to budge even one slat. Finally, using the hammer and crowbar, she smashes the slats, sending splintered wood flying everywhere. Tabby peeks out from the towel, still trembling and purring. The leg is mangled. I wonder how long the blood flow has been restricted. Could the leg really be salvaged? I'm prepared for the officer to put it in the truck, knowing it's a lost cause and take it away to be euthanized. It must be a difficult job sometimes. I can see how much she loves animals.

"What can you do?"

"Well, I'll take it to the 24-hour veterinary ER. There's an on-call vet." She looks sincere and hopeful. It turns out too late to make a later flight. I'm exhausted and drag into the Hilton near the airport. It will be a short night as I'm rebooked on a 6 a.m. flight home. Just after landing the phone is ringing. It's Mona.

"The veterinary tech called this morning saying the kitten had surgery and didn't lose its leg. No broken bones. Just some tissue damage that needed stitches. He's one tough kitten, and the vet expects him to pull through. We're amazed. That little cat has never stopped purring."

I can hear Lexi in the background, "Mom, Mom, tell Miss Talkington."

"Oh, says Mona, we're getting a new kitten. Bruno's gone."

16 Humility at Gate 77

With Humility Comes Wisdom
— Proverbs 11:2

THIS WEEK I'VE BEEN IN California surveying a Board and Care Home. Board and Care homes became the state's answer to deinstitutionalization. Typically, these homes are integrated into residential neighborhoods and are home to 6-8 residents with mental health challenges or developmental disabilities. Various other terms for such homes are used depending on the state. Residential care, community-based care, adult foster homes, and developmentally disabled residences.

The history of mental health and psychiatric treatment isn't pretty. Too many institutionalized people suffered abuse, neglect, and mistreatment. American society had a tough time reconciling that members of our population had imperfections and were irreverently referred to as flawed, crippled, freaks, *maniacs* or just not right in the head. It was deemed best to keep the person out of sight and remove the visible reminders of weakness and frailty from public view. Institutions were permanent residences for those with birth injuries (cerebral palsy); what we now know as genetic disorders like mongolism (Down's Syndrome); epilepsy, deformities of the skull - water on the brain (hydrocephalus); abnormally small skulls (microcephaly); or Sydenham chorea a movement disorder, (originally called St. Vitus Dance) a neuromuscular movement disorder caused by a strep infection or rheumatic fever in childhood, and what we now know as bipolar disorder or schizophrenia. Theoretically, *back then*, it might have even been possible that those with severe autism would have been institutionalized. Across the country institutionalization met with opposition and support.

"We knew something was wrong when our daughter Debbie was born. We tried to care for her at home. By the time she was four it was too much. Our only choice was to put her in an institution – the State Home and Training School. She's forty-five now and has been lovingly cared for by her nurses. They are the only parents Debbie's ever known. She cannot walk and needs to be fed. What will happen to her?"

Others proclaimed. "They're letting the crazies out on the streets."

When deinstitutionalization began 50 years ago, California mistakenly relied on community treatment facilities that were never built. Instead, Board and Care Homes were opened in an attempt to meet the law.

In most states the state health department is the designated regulatory body that conducts onsite evaluations and grants licenses to operate. This isn't the usual type of survey visit I normally do. But owners of this Board and Care chose to obtain certification and licensing through my employer, a national organization, that is approved by California. In essence California has subcontracted the site survey to us. There are some additional California-specific regulations (standards) that my colleagues and I are trained to evaluate. As wearing as it is, I like the challenge. Considering the history of institutionalization, I love meeting residents who are leading happy, successful, and productive lives. Many residents in these settings attend day programs or have jobs in the community or sheltered workshops.

An agency receives a handsome monthly stipend for each resident. It's a legitimate amount given the variety of services they are supposed to provide. Board and Care ownership and management isn't an easy business to operate, and companies may own more than one in an effort to make a profit. Sometimes multiple ownerships are too much strain. At the time of my visit there were 4,000 Board and Care residences.

"We sure get a lot of popsicles," confides Maddie when I ask her about meals. Maddie's a young adult-onset diabetic with controlled epilepsy who's unable to live on her own. No wonder she's having trouble with high blood sugars. A typical menu item twice a week is fish sticks and fries. Devon shows me the room he shares with Dillon. Each of them takes the bus daily to attend an adult day program.

"I'm afraid of Dillon," Devon says. "He punches holes in the walls. I want to change rooms, but they won't let me."

Dillon says, "I get a lot of time outs."

Annabelle is sitting in the dayroom googly-eyed watching television. A bulletin board lists available activities, some that require supervision. She needs help with personal care as do the others.

"I like to play Chinese checkers," she says, "but the nurse is always too busy."

None of them could remember having vegetables.

"If we could have it, I'd like zucchini," announced Annabelle and Maddie simultaneously.

I was reluctant to leave after observing and talking with the residents. They were not in immediate danger, but the situation had to be addressed. Given my findings it was necessary to notify the State health department to ensure that someone would be sent, unannounced the next day. It was a difficult two-day visit with several serious citations requiring submission of a Plan of Correction to the state within 48 hours and a follow-up site visit from our organization within 60 days. In addition to reporting to the state I also reported findings and observations to my supervisor about the outcome of the visit. Visits like these can be discouraging. I remind myself that there are many, many Board and Care residences that pass onsite surveys with excellence. Many receive awards.

It's another snarly Friday night at the airport. Everybody has had a difficult week too.

"I DON'T know when I'll be home. Looks like I'll miss Jake's program," yells a husband into his cell phone, above the din. He's already ripped his tie off while he's talking to his wife.

"NOW what's the holdup?!?" echoes an angry voice amid the unruly crowd at Gate 77. Finally, the overdue flight from Florida pulls into the gate; two hours since its expected arrival.

"Folks, we're trying to get passengers off as quickly as we can and then we'll get you on to your destinations. Please be patient. Before we can board, we need to deplane passengers who need a little assistance."

Renewed boos and a rush to the podium ensues. Fingers are being pointed and fists pounded. I often take this Friday night flight in my 100,000-mile road warrior life and recognize the usual cantankerous complainers.

Jaws drop, people stare, and silence descends in the boarding area. A couple in their fifties, and a helper, push six young disabled adults in wheelchairs up the ramp to the gate area headed to the disabled bathrooms to change diapers and fill water bottles.

"We're a foster family for the disabled," says the young helper as she passes me. "We live all together in a large, lovely care home in Bellaire."

The troupe is sporting Mickey Mouse ears and waving Disney World balloons tied to their wrists. Everyone is laughing and singing *It's a Small World Afterall*. Clapping and cheering replaces grumbling. What a finale to a bad week. This is what deinstitutionalization is all about. The man next to me, a familiar Friday night fellow traveler leaned over,

"I will never ever complain again. I just got a wake-up call from God about humility."

17 Keebler Elves Keep Watch

....there sat at the kitchen table, she found three little elves. Oh they were eating and drinking and having a merry old time.....
— from *Merry Old Folk Tales* by Athey Thompson

CAROL WILSON BELIEVES Keebler elves break into her house at night and cause mischief. Moving objects to other rooms and hiding them. Keebler bakery has been a landmark in northwest Denver since 1962 when the plant was built in the field next to the Wilson's. Until 2001 when the plant closed aroma from the factory filled the neighborhood with scents of Pecan Sandies and Club Crackers. Although most of us are familiar with Snap, Crackle, and Pop of Rice Crispy fame Elf lore holds that ad man Leo Burnett created the elves for Keebler in 1969. I doubt that J.J. Keebler, the first head Elf to be created, would approve of this behavior. Uncommonly good. *A little elfin magic goes a long way.* A famous tag line implies not only are the cookies uncommonly good so are the elves.

"Those little devils. Oh, they're cute but they crawl under the fence from the plant. Look here. My toothbrush was in the silverware drawer this morning."

Carol is a new patient in my assigned home care neighborhood. I'm visiting because she's been having panic attacks, shortness of breath, chest pain and heart failure. I'm completely unaware these symptoms can also be related to Widower's syndrome or

Broken Heart Syndrome. Carol was the quintessential 1950s June Cleaver housewife. Looking at photos on the credenza, Mr. Wilson was a dead ringer for Ward Cleaver. Sixty-two years they lived their married life together in this typical post WWII neighborhood of brick bungalow style homes with manicured grass lawns. She's alone now in that cookie cutter style residence; one floor plan, three-bedrooms, one bath, kitchen with an arched cut through to a formal dining room and living room. America was still on the cusp of needing family rooms to accommodate watching TV. No basement to send the kids to either. A one car detached brick garage protected the latest model Ford or Chrysler that was dutifully washed and polished on Saturday mornings with the garden hose.

Harold and Carol had been sweethearts since she was 15 and he 19. Inseparable till the day he died six months ago. Before they married in 1948, they were often in the mountains fishing. Saturday evening had always been date night. Harold spent his paycheck paying for Carol to ride the Loop-O-Plane at Lakeside. Before Larry was born, they danced in the Trocadero Ballroom at Elitch Gardens or attended a play at Elitch Summer Theatre on Saturday. Before curtain call, they enjoyed a picnic supper at one of the quaint wooden tables hidden in the flower gardens. They belonged to a couples' bowling league and joined a set of friends for cards on Friday nights. After Larry graduated and went off to college, Harold and Carol started an annual tradition of driving to Las Vegas to play the slots.

Each morning and evening, Monday through Friday during the family years Harold took the Tramway bus to his 9-5 job as a loan officer at Colorado National Bank in downtown Denver. At the end of the workday, you'd see him walking up the sidewalk to the back door. He would wave to workers exiting the parking lot at the Keebler cookie factory as the ovens shut down for the day. After removing his polished Thom McCann shoes in the mudroom, he would give Carol a peck on the cheek in answer to *how was your day dear?* Sitting at the kitchen table they each talked about their day. Meatloaf and baked potatoes on Monday. Pork chops and gravy with canned peas and lime green Jell-O on Wednesday nights. They had an ordered life. Saturday, they walked to Dutch Boy donuts in the Shoppette across from Keebler for coffee and old fashioned buttermilk donuts. The rest of the morning was spent washing the car, mowing the lawn, and trimming the edges with shears: no weed whackers. Washing came with Monday and Tuesday was ironing. Carol shopped for groceries at Piggly Wiggly on Thursdays. She left them at the store and Harold picked them up after dinner and paid the bill. Sundays could be no other day but family day. Sausage and pancake breakfast after Mass. Pot roast dinner with Waldorf salad preceded a drive to the mountains or an afternoon visiting aging relatives still alive.

That was family life in the 1950s and 1960s. Most wives stayed home. Husbands worked in jobs they would retire from after forty years of employment with guaranteed pension plans. Husbands not only mowed the lawn but also managed family finances; approving major purchases and investments; paying monthly bills; and balancing the checkbook. Six months ago, when Harold passed, Carol had never driven a car. She was terrified thinking about what she would have to take over and do on her own for the first time. Shaking her head and then her fist in the empty house she yells at the Elves,

"Why did he go and leave me?" She's lost the love of her life and grieves alone.

After visiting Carol for a couple of weeks I noticed curious behaviors. When I arrive at midday all the curtains are drawn, and she sneaks window to window peering out. A wet load of laundry is left in the washing machine. TV dinners are stacked in the freezer. She eats cereal for dinner she tells me.

"Are you expecting someone?"

"Shhh, you have to be really quiet. Don't let them get in. It's the Elves. They know Harold isn't here."

Carol's Medicare approval for 60 days home care is about to end, and her physical symptoms have cleared. She understands how to take her new medications; her ankles aren't as swollen; a positive sign that the heart failure is subsiding. Now I notice she's opened the living room drapes before my visit. She's learned to drive around the block but doesn't get out to Piggly Wiggly. Instead, Larry brings weekly groceries, including heart healthy foods that go untouched. She hasn't stayed in touch with their bowling and cards friends. She hasn't said anything more about elves. A week before my last visit she asks.

"Do you want to see something?" She walks me into the bedroom to her chest of drawers where a loaded .38 revolver handgun is hidden in the underwear.

"Nobody is going to get in here. Those pesky elves won't bother me anymore."

I'm shocked and don't know what to say, much less do. The previous year a home health nurse was shot and killed during a domestic violence altercation while she was in a home. All of us still can't believe it. Over the next year, for the first time, policies were put into place addressing guns in the home. Mandatory staff training on personal safety, self-defense and how to diffuse dangerous or potentially volatile situations became a requirement. Gun violence that we see these days was unimaginable back then, only hunters owned rifles. Police officers had holstered revolvers. As a child, I was taught to call policemen peace officers. U.S. gun owners possessed almost 400 million guns in 2018. One of the most tragic outcomes is the rise in suicides and accidental deaths caused by guns.

"Carol, let's leave it in the drawer and I'll give Larry a call."

"Hi Mom, tell me about the gun in your drawer."

"Well, those Elves seem to be in the house all the time; they're driving me buggy. I remembered your dad had it in his drawer."

"Let's do this. I get off work in half an hour and will come over. Your nurse will stay with you till I get there. Just leave the gun in the drawer. Don't touch it."

"Okay, I'm glad you're coming. Maybe you can talk to those Elves." Larry arrived as planned.

"Mom, the gun will be better at my house. I'm going to take it when I go. I talked to those Elves and guess what? They were just watching over you to keep you safe now that Dad's gone."

Larry and I discussed the implications and what to do next. I scheduled an appointment with her doctor for early the next morning and Larry went with her. Her physician suspected she was suffering from a temporary dementia that caused paranoia, resulting from depression and grieving. This is what contributed to the panic attacks and signs of heart failure. He prescribed an antidepressant and the agency's medical social worker was scheduled to visit to help Carol find ways to reengage with life. I saw Carol four more visits after that.

It was only later that home care nurses began to recognize the symptoms of Broken Heart Syndrome. Widowhood Effect, Silent Grief. This phenomenon isn't an old wives' tale about older adults who have an increased risk of dying shortly after a spouse. Most early studies revolved around defining the symptoms, associated effects on the immune system and prediction of how long the syndrome could be expected to last. Grief after the death of a spouse can be profound. Nowadays treatment is directed at grief and loss. As happened with Carol, antidepressants are prescribed in addition to mental health workers to provide widowers and widows become engaged in life again. A year later I was in the neighborhood to visit another patient and drove by the Wilson house. Carol was backing out of the garage.

"Grief is the price you pay for love," said a grieving Queen Elizabeth II about her beloved Philip after 74 years of marriage when he died in April 2021. "He has left a huge void in my life."

At her death in 2022, just a little over a year after his, a news headline spoke the truth "Ultimately Queen Elizabeth died of a broken heart."

18 Everyone Needs a Spot

"You cannot separate the old furniture from the memories and the memories from the old furniture!"
— Mehmet Murat Ildan

As a person gets older the more they need a Spot. By the time they reach the seventh decade of life and certainly by the time they become octogenarians they spend more time in their Spot than anywhere else. *X marks the Spot*, so the saying goes. A Spot assumes the identity of its occupant and becomes the heartbeat of the home. Each Spot is as individual and as unique as its owner. I'm not certain that all home care nurses recognize their patient's Spot. Most likely they see it but don't understand what a Spot signifies. So many of those intuitive assessment skills of home healthcare nurses have become a lost art. Nonetheless, I'm quite sure I've seen hundred of Spots. A person's Spot is where a home care visit is likely to begin and end.

"Door's open come in," Harriet Bannister calls out.

There she is waiting for me in her Spot, an overstuffed velvet recliner chair with tea towels on the arms. TV trays flank the chair. One holds a steaming mug of coffee on a crocheted coaster. A Kleenex box is atop a Daily Devotional booklet that is atop a half-read letter from her sister in Dubuque. The stack reminds me of Jenga blocks. On the bottom is a list of emergency numbers, next of kin, and healthcare providers. An assortment of prescription bottles, arthritis strength Tylenol and a half-squeezed tube of joint liniment intermingle on the other tray. Used tissues have missed the waste basket at her feet. Cataracts. A pile of unopened mail - snail mail, subscriptions, solicitations from philanthropic organizations, bills, letters, and magazines form another Jenga pile on the floor. A leather-bound address book with frayed letter tabs lists contacts from decades ago, most of whom are deceased. It's stuffed with scraps of paper listing more recent contacts and is close by on the coffee table in front of her. Harriet's portable phone has become lodged between the seat cushion and chair arm.

A floor lamp better suited for a visitation room at a mortuary, beams down over her left shoulder illuminating the Spot. A large screen TV holds a prominent place on the wall across from the Spot. Her twelve-year-old grandson has written out step- by-step instructions for using the remote. Wherever there is a Spot a magnifying glass and flashlight aren't far away. A Spot is often where a patient sleeps overnight and snoozes during the day, or vice versa. Meals are eaten in the Spot. This personal cocoon of protected life is where vital signs are measured, skin assessed, aches and pains evaluated, symptoms of chronic diseases are checked out as well as possible side effects of medications. Starting at the Spot can lead a nurse to tell-tale signs of how well your home care patient is really doing.

Harriet and I go over medications. *What was Big Pharma thinking of?!* I'm absolutely convinced that prescriptions are uniquely designed to frustrate anyone over fifty. Pills are either so small and slippery they pinch out of arthritic fingers or are so big as to be gagged on or spit out. Either way pills end up in and around the Spot without the person realizing it. And we wonder why a person's blood pressure seems to be going up not down. Nurses are most relieved when medications are organized in a plastic medication planner designed to separate medications into days of the week and times of day.

Once, a patient of mine who had retired from being a carpenter built a garage workshop where screws and nails were organized in baby food jars. He decided to experiment with baby food jars for pills. He proceeded to empty original prescription bottles into individual jars and labeled them with names and times using a magic marker. It was a disaster. Harriet prefers leaving her pills in their bottles instead of using a planner. In the 2000s automatic medication dispensing devices were supposed to be the be all end all to medication compliance but were never very successful.

Dehydration, a common cause of urinary tract infections (UTI) leads to falls and subsequently emergent care or hospitalization. So, every Spot must have a quart water pitcher. On one visit I caught Harriet dumping out her water in a nearby potted plant.

"Rats, you caught me," she confesses. "Some days I feel like you're trying to drown me."

"But have you had a UTI recently?" I remind her.

"Harriet, you look good today, you're up and dressed. Have you had breakfast?" She avoids the question.

"I always look forward to your visit. Oh, I'll eat a banana when you go."

It's possible to find empty TV dinner trays squirreled away in a Spot.

Every Spot has hidden dangers.

"How did you get that bruise on you left arm?"

"Darn it. Went to get up from the chair and fell over. Tripped on my lap blanket and scraped my arm on the coffee table."

If I could impress anything on nurses old and new it would be to find the patient's Spot. It will tell you a lot.

A Spot can be potential breeding ground for Compulsive Hoarding Disorder. A life of traumatic experiences forms psychological wounds that beg protection and comfort with *Things*. Everywhere. Metaphorically speaking, a person's Spot takes over every inch of the home like a pandemic. It's a distressing situation for home healthcare nurses. Attempts to cure the situation are rarely successful. Serious hoarding predisposes a person to health and safety concerns such as fire hazards, tripping and falls, and health code violations. A corresponding social reaction also occurs. Hoarders become socially marginalized and isolated because people blame them for their situation. There is the assumption that hoarders *need to get rid of it all*. Hoarding is a complex and complicated mental health disorder.

At each visit to Edith Waring's apartment, I wiggle my way through a cavern of six-foot-high boxes and plastic storage tubs that clog the hallways.

Kitchen cupboards are crammed with not one but twenty cans of spaghetti, twelve cans of chili, and a dozen high fructose syrup Bartlett pears. The cabinet doors won't close, and an avalanche of cans is threatening to tumble out. Many cans are outdated or have bulging lids. In the dark recesses of the refrigerator a host of microscopic flora turns vegetables black and blue and smelly. Nurses worry about accidental food poisoning. Given no available storage space, spices, potholders, kitchen towels, paper plates, and napkins are stored on top of the electric stove burners. As the control dials aren't visible it's a perfect scenario for an impromptu kitchen fire. A Mixmaster blender, bread maker, two Keurig coffee makers, an electric can opener and a toaster oven claim what minimal counter space there is. A dishwasher that needs repair is the resting place for washed and unwashed dishes. Seven large quart bottles of dishing washing detergent, multiple spray bottles of Lysol and cans of Comet cleanser have tumbled from the cabinet below the sink where there are mouse droppings.

Clothes racks on backs of doors are bursting with hangers of clothes because three closets are jammed with vintage styles from the 60s, eleven purses, twenty-two pairs of shoes, and fifteen hats. A dozen sweaters are stuffed under the bed suffering a recent infestation of bedbugs. On top of the mattress are twelve pairs of jeans and twenty-six t-shirts that commemorate places visited, and events attended. Teton National Park, Super Bowl 50,

Everglades, 5K Labor Day Run, I Summited the Peak, Grandma of Ten and I Love My Siamese.

A dining table has been taken over by plastic four-drawer storage containers. Several drawers are overflowing with enough supplies to support an art studio. Tubes of oils and watercolors, crayons, color pencils and ink pens and coloring books. Other drawers hold stickers, ribbons, bows, a glue gun, wrapping paper and a collection of gift bags. Another storage container holds scrapbooking supplies and knitting needles and yarn. Dining chairs have become dead zones with years and years of unopened mail and overdue statements that have gone to collection for unpaid balances. The living room wall displays dusty music cassettes and CDs and VHS tapes in storage holders. A defunct computer sits idly supporting a box of five extension cords, four power strips, six pair of sunglasses, seven phone chargers, an eyeglass repair kit, and a gallon Ziploc of thirty AAA batteries.

Edith's four-wheeled walker, the kind that the seat folds down, is too wide to get into the bathroom, so she parks it at the end of the hallway and navigates around a dirty clothes hamper and cat commode to a vanity where she steadies herself to get into a toilet/shower room.

Each visit Edith sits in her Spot and I complete my assessment from a webbed lawn chair used for guests. In these situations, nurses leave their nursing bag in the car since there's no safe place to put it. Instead, I put my stethoscope around my neck and sanitizer and a pair of gloves in my pocket. I'm relieved that Edith has her own thermometer and blood pressure cuff. If we can find them.

Dealing with such complicated homes can become troubling for home healthcare nurses. We want to make it all better for every patient. For the Ediths of our lives, it's tempting to want to take everything to the dumpsters and start over. However, compulsive buying goes hand in hand with compulsive hoarding. So, thanks to the presence of Amazon, the clutter would reappear within a month, and she would be overdrawn in the bank. Even stripping and cleaning can't cure the disorder.

It's an agonizing decision to have to make a referral to Social Services because the home environment is so dangerous. I couldn't ignore the cluttered or blocked pathways. Edith already had several falls because of blocked pathways clogged with *stuff*. When bedbugs were so thick that Edit had bites all over her arms. She had put out several mouse houses. I knew I had to do something. I just kept hoping we'd be able to gradually clean and address the safety hazards. It was the kitchen fire that was the tipping point. A burner on the stove was inadvertently turned on and a dishtowel and stack of paper bags on the stovetop caught fire. There was smoke damage and building management gave her a final warning about safety. Calling Social Services was something I had to do. A county caseworker recruited and coordinated assistance for much needed cleaning, scrubbing, and painting. Trash dumpsters were filled. A Medical Social Worker familiar with home care and specializing in grief and its relationship to hoarding visited her over the course of eight months. I visited one last time when nursing care was no longer needed. Six weeks later I received a follow-up call from Social Services. A group of friends from her church had managed to reduce the number of piles and tubs. She was gifting her hobby supplies to a community art program.

It's easy to be judgmental, to criticize hoarders for not doing something about their situation. Many have lost friends and family because no one wants to visit them. This is one of those times when home care nurses have to reconcile that sometimes we just can't make everything all better. But we can call upon community resources and other caring professionals to at least reduce or mitigate the circumstances.

There are reasons a hoarder's home looks like it does. Over the years their Spot just grew too big to manage or let go of.

19 What Wreath Are You?

Make the most of yourself…. For that is all there is of you.
—Ralph Waldo Emerson

FUTURISTS IN THE 1980s and 1990s predicted startling changes ahead for aging adults in the autumn of their lives. The Baby Boomer Generation (1946—1964.) could not comprehend that natural aging had its many manifestations that would affect the home in which they lived. As the seventieth decade of their lives came and went a familiar quote began to circulate *getting old is hell.*

Now, getting older is fashionably called *eldering* as the way to live out your remaining days. Where do aging seniors live nowadays? Those same futurists, in capitalistic fashion, not only predicted but created a vast profitable, muti-billion-dollar industry. Home is called many things these days. Assisted Living Facility has been replaced by Assisted Living Community. Lifestyle Community has evolved from Independent Living. 55+ Active Living Communities (apartments or condos) were the rage of the 1990s. Aging occurs everywhere as does the ability to live independently, or not. As a practicing home healthcare nurse, I was right in the thick of these sweeping trends. Making visits in large senior apartment complexes became an adventure. Decorative wreaths, crafted from all types of arts and crafts, proudly hung on many apartment doors on both sides of a hallway. Each door, like a prologue to a novel, introduced a resident's life story.

Ornithologist

Lydia Wheatley's wreath featured miniature red paper mâché cardinals, blue jays and white doves accentuated by wheat stalks. The first visit I saw her eye through the security peephole. The birds look almost real. She opened the door unexpectedly and I tumbled in.

"Shhh, walk slowly behind me." She whispers. She tiptoes to a sliding glass patio door looking out to an enclosed courtyard. Maple, ash, and blue spruce trees draw wrens, chickadees, and finches. A wing chair strategically positioned to catch all the action in the courtyard, is surrounded by stacks of birding books. Roger Tory Peterson, Ken Kaufman, and David Sibley field guides. *The men to go to*. She asks if I've discovered Noah Stryker's book *Thing With Feathers*. How did she intuit that I'm a birder?

"Here, use these." She nudges me with a pair of binoculars. "Look up there at that little Downy Woodpecker. See how he hops around the tree trunk sporting his red crown?"

Weekly for the next two weeks I followed her progress after open heart surgery. Lydia is a well-known retired ornithologist who led birding tours around the world. Accenting the wall behind the couch were reproductions of ornithologist John James Audubon's famous watercolors of birds. Lydia reminds me of a little wren hopping about.

"And this, Mrs. Wheatley? Where is that? A framed 1950s enlarged photo overlooks the dining area.

"Oh, I grew up on a wheat ranch in eastern Washington. That's where I got my love of birds."

Rah Rah Rah – Celebrating Football Season

As Assisted Living Communities grew larger in size and numbers of residents, intersecting hallways and multiple elevators could be confusing.

"Turn left as you come off the elevator in the south wing where Midge Turner's wreath of cotton bolls hangs. Follow that hall to the end. We're apartment 201. Can't miss it."

At O'Sullivan's a wreath made of grapevine branches spray painted green is adorned with miniature Notre Dame University pennants. Anne and Tom O'Sullivan are a long way from their Maryland home of sixty-four years. Their only child Shaun is a prominent criminal practice lawyer in Colorado. As Tom and Anne became more in need of help, Shaun and his wife Karen were increasingly traveling back and forth twice monthly to Frederick, MD to manage Anne's declining health. Finally, a decision was made to move his parents to Colorado. Tom took the move in stride primarily because he was still able to play golf, have lunch once a week and go to Bar Association events with his son. Both were Notre Dame law school alumni. Tom joined a men's discussion group at the Assisted Living on Fridays. For Anne it was probably the worst thing that ever happened in her life.

"Why can't I just die. I never wanted to get this old. Why did he move us here? I suppose you saw that disgusting green wreath. Oh, nooo…. I couldn't bring my precious silver tea set but that stupid wreath!"

All I could do was listen. Little by little I began to draw her out by asking her to tell me of her early childhood in Maryland; the year she was presented to society at the debutante ball; belonging to a bridge club; entertaining law school faculty and their wives, chairing committees; president of the Altar and Rosary Society; attending art exhibitions. What a foreign life here.

Moving out of state is especially difficult for seniors even if it's their choice. Making the move to Colorado was definitely not Anne's choice. For every senior, making a move to a final home can be deeply traumatizing. Many factors necessarily influence the decision. Most often the reason is proximity to adult children, family, or others who can facilitate or assist with health and medical needs and managing finances. Many also become primary caregivers who assume personal care of their parent. On my weekly companion visits to Anne, we listened to audiobooks, or I read her favorite book or poetry aloud. She liked the classics. We finished Pride and Prejudice two weeks before she passed on her ninety-seventh birthday.

Jokester

Along with wreaths, doors often have other clues to a resident's identity. Dorothy Wichers' door gets a chuckle from passersby. She's a jokester. At Halloween a life-size mannequin costumed as a witch has slammed into Dorothy's door while in flight. A broom drags between her skinny legs in black and white striped leotards. Her crooked warty nose pokes out from below the brim of a black pointy Gandolph hat. A green rubber frog hangs from her wrist. It's easy to imagine the smell of toads, spiders, and chicken livers boiling in a hidden cauldron. A white mist swirls out the door as she opens it. Dry ice in a bucket behind the door. At Thanksgiving, a trio of Tom Turkeys gobble when the door is opened. At St. Patrick's a banner displays felt leprechauns dancing around a pot of gold. A jig plays when anyone uses the door knocker. Every holiday her sense of humor is greatly anticipated and she's the talk of the hallway.

Fisherman

A perfectly mounted 18″ rainbow trout, tail at a flip, its wide maw open in the motion of making a strike greets visitors at Jeremy Fisher's door. Fly-fishing rods stand in a corner of the apartment and two stuffed Canada geese perch on the air conditioner jutting from the wall. Jeremy retired two years ago after forty years as a Fish and Game warden with the State Wildlife Division. His knee replacement was successful and he's looking ahead to getting out to the lake again.

African Wildlife

Dottie Wilde, doyenne of fifth floor, is proud of her African savannah door featuring select National Geographic photos of giraffes, wildebeests, lions, and zebras. Jerry, her husband, was a wildlife photographer, and they made several trips to Africa in the 1970s and 80s. Their photo albums were lost to an apartment fire last year. Honoring the memory, I take my place on the zebra skin couch with a five-foot poofy stuffed toy giraffe looking over my shoulder as I start my visit.

Theologian

Martin Newberry earned his Doctorate in Theology at a historic Catholic Jesuit University in the Northwest after completing undergraduate degrees in philosophy and ethics. In addition to teaching at a private university he wrote essays and editorials for noted publications and was a much sought-after lecturer. Widowed at a young age he'd maintained a suburban home where he could entertain colleagues and a book group. After a long career he retired to a modest apartment where he could write. Students had aways suspected he was somewhat of a mystic. Martin became reclusive when the pandemic occurred. Soon intellectually provocative essays and editorials appeared on his door as well as biographies and commentary on the lives of various philosophers and statesmen. Unfortunately, building management received complaints from neighbors on second floor. Essays that he regularly posted on his door were too existential, a curiosity that didn't suit everyone's taste. Others missed the mental stimulation. It was suggested that someone should buy him a wreath because the door was too bare.

I've hung the St. Patrick's Day Wreath on the door of my apartment just above the *Blessed Are the Peacemakers* Hermitage plaque. It was here, tucked away and quiet, where I brought

Home Is Everywhere to a close after nine years in the making. The stories have been told and it's time to be done. The purple roller bag suitcase has retired to the back of the closet. While writing, I played out the people and places once again; like flashbacks in a movie and I am content...................

May All Your Roads Lead Home
— Dominic Moriarity

www.ingramcontent.com/pod-product-compliance
Lightning Source LLC
Chambersburg PA
CBHW051530120626
46551CB00012B/1160